Top-down Programming using Turbo Pascal

A case study approach

Alan Clark
Margaret Williams

Loughborough College

ARNOLD

A member of the Hodder Headline Group
LONDON • SYDNEY • AUCKLAND

To our parents

First published in Great Britain 1997 by Arnold,
a member of the Hodder Headline Group,
338 Euston Road, London NW1 3BH

Brtish Library Cataloguing in Publication Data
A catalogue record for this book is available from the British Library

Library of Congress Cataloging-in-Publication Data
A catalog record for this book is available from the Library of Congress

ISBN 0 340 66287 5

Typeset in 10/12pt Garamond by Wearset, Boldon, Tyne and Wear
Printed and bound in Great Britain by J. W. Arrowsmith Ltd, Bristol

Turbo Pascal is a registered trademark
of Borland International Inc.

Contents

1
Introduction

How to use this book

This is a book about programming.

This might be an obvious statement to make. Are there not many books about programming? There are, but each takes a somewhat different approach to programming.

Inevitably, a programming book will teach a particular programming language. In the case of this book, the language chosen is Pascal, but the skills that you should be able to acquire should be general skills. Programming is an opportunity to develop problem solving skills. Having worked through the material in this book, you should have a very good grasp of the broad principles of programming. Applying these ideas in another programming language should then be a relatively straightforward matter.

The philosophy behind this book is that the programming language is the medium, but the message is that programs can be used to solve real problems.

All programming languages are, by their nature, very unforgiving to users who write programs. The rules of the language must be followed exactly, otherwise the language compiler will indicate the dreaded 'syntax error'.

The aim of this book is not primarily to teach coding in a specific language (Pascal). The aim of this book is not to teach programming concepts using a suitable language. The aim of this book, rather, is to teach general problem solving techniques, using programming concepts and a suitable language (Pascal) as vehicles for this.

Many traditional courses see programming as mainly a mechanical coding exercise. Programs are presented as recipes to be followed. Early exercises emphasise attention to detail and readers might spend hours on 'pretty' layout. Yet this approach can neglect actual problem solving skills.

Because program design cannot be practised without a knowledge of the language rules (syntax), many books describe simple problems at first for which the algorithms are trivial. This can mean that ideas such as top-down programming and structured design are given too little emphasis. Readers can usually cope with this approach, but still regard it as primarily learning the language. When a second language is taught and the same programming concepts are mentioned again, the general ideas may begin to take hold so long as they are not submerged in language features and syntax.

The approach taken in this book puts the whole emphasis on problem solving.

Part of that emphasis is to use from the start an approach to programming known as 'top-down'. This involves breaking problems into smaller, more manageable sections. In this book, those more manageable sections are implemented as procedures, with these being used from the start. Initially, you will mainly be using procedures that are ready-written, but from the start it is important that you understand *what* they do, and perhaps even more importantly, *what* data they need in order to do it. You may not, at the early stage understand *how* a procedure does a job, but appreciating a procedure as a 'black box' into which data is fed, which carries out tasks, and which returns updated data, is a key concept.

This approach to top-down problem solving means that, from the very commencement of the teaching material in this book, you are thinking about procedures which are the natural components of which programs are made. In early case studies, you will see a problem broken down and the relevant procedures provided. A little later, you will see the problem broken down and you must provide the procedures yourself. At the third stage, you will break down the problems for yourself. It is therefore important from the start to consider how the data passes to and from a procedure and how it acts on that data.

You may find this approach interesting but difficult, as this book looks at realistic problems from the start. Your difficulties may not be with the programming concepts or the coding, but with the problem solving itself.

The libraries of code

At the core of the methods in this book lies the idea of a library of code, which is referred to as a unit in Turbo Pascal. This allows the authors to provide ready-written parts of code that are then used by you as a reader. To get the most out of this book, indeed to get much at all out of this book, you will need to be an active learner. This means that you will need to do the exercises. This is the only way in which you will see the ideas described working in practice.

The libraries that are supplied on disk are described later in this chapter. Because you are provided with ready-written code, you will see many examples of good practice in coding. When good practice is later described, you will perhaps feel that the description is an obvious one, as you will have picked up so many ideas by reading examples. This is rather like the manner in which we learn a natural language, such as English. From birth, because we are surrounded by good examples of the use of the rules of the language, we therefore begin to see the use of the language rules (however odd they may be) as natural.

With the approach used here, that of providing libraries of ready-written code, the aim is to give you the tools you need to solve realistic problems right from the start. This 'toolkit' approach should encourage you to see similarities between different problems. Even the early programs, despite consisting of only a few lines of code, solve interesting problems by calling procedures from a library to perform more complicated processes. Initially units are provided which you will be asked to compile without looking at their contents. Later, you will inspect the contents of the libraries, and later still you will write your own.

Having written a set of libraries for a class of problems, such as handling dates, you can use these units to solve similar but different problems. This is what some of the later exercises seek to reinforce. Well-designed programs should stimulate the production of libraries that can be used in similar problems.

At any stage, more advanced ideas can still be provided pre-written. Re-use of code is also encouraged.

This approach is not without its difficulties. You may feel 'thrown in at the deep end'. There are very few books that take anything like this approach. If you have your own machine and read the manuals, you will see little that relates to what is done in the early chapters of this book. Manuals are designed for reference and work best for looking something up when you have grasped the main concepts.

If you try skipping a few chapters of this book, you will almost certainly become completely lost. There are several reasons for this. New concepts are introduced throughout the various chapters, and then may be used in any of the later chapters. The summaries at the start of each chapter are there to help you appreciate what is covered in the chapter, and what you will need to know to gain the benefit from the chapter's contents. Inevitably, particularly early on, there are a lot of diverse ideas covered in each chapter, so the summaries may not describe them all in detail. Another effect of the approach taken here is that later chapters may depend on code that you have been asked to produce as exercises in previous chapters. Without this code in working form, you will be unable to tackle some of the later work.

You may have browsed through a number of programming books in an effort to choose an appropriate one to buy so that you can learn about programming. If you do this, you will find many references to ideas such as 'Jackson Structured Programming', 'structured English', 'pseudocode', 'flowcharts' and 'object orientation'. Each of these is one of a wide range of techniques advocated over the last few decades for problem solving and program design. Many have their drawbacks, and most programmers will use a variety of these techniques where appropriate. For the designs of the programs used in this book, many of the techniques identified are weak because they do not put enough emphasis on the access to and manipulation of the limited amounts of data which are to be handled by procedures and functions.

One of the important concepts in modern programming is that of 'object oriented' programming. Such an approach is not taken in this book, but the approach can be described as 'object-compatible'. If you take your studies further, you may be introduced to objects, and at that point you may well say, 'but that's only a version of what I've always done'.

The structure of this book

After this introductory chapter, which describes the philosophy behind the book and its approach to programming, Chapter 2 describes the Turbo Pascal system. Readers who are familiar with features of Turbo Pascal such as the editor and compiler could skip this chapter.

In Chapters 3 to 10, programming concepts and their particular implementations in Turbo Pascal are successively revealed. Each chapter does this through developing a case study which illustrates the ideas in a practical way. Some of these case studies are returned to in more detail in later chapters. As part of the exercises in each chapter you will build up your own library of useful code in a utility unit called 'utils'.

Each of the chapters from 3 to 10 includes summary information at the start. This explains which concepts have been previously covered and it is therefore assumed that you understand. It also explains those items which should have been written in the utilities library. The summary then details the new concepts introduced in the chapter and the new items for the utilities library which will be produced as a result of the exercises in the chapter.

Chapter 11 describes some projects which could be used to practise the ideas introduced. There are no new ideas introduced in this chapter.

Chapters 12 and 13 describe some more advanced features of Turbo Pascal such as graphics and sets to give a more complete picture of Turbo Pascal. Some programming structures which are not mentioned in previous chapters are described to give you a fuller picture of Pascal.

Various appendices are included to help you access reference information.

Why choose Turbo Pascal?

If the important thing about learning programming is problem solving, not the details of a particular language, why choose Turbo Pascal?

At the core of Turbo Pascal is the library approach. These are therefore used from the start. They are so fundamental to good programming style that they are not included as an after-thought. Anybody learning programming should learn good habits from the start. The philosophy should also be that if good, tested code exists which can do a job, then it should be used. To quote the old cliché, programmers need not re-invent the wheel.

In this book, there are three types of units (also known as libraries). There are many ready-written units that are provided as part of Turbo Pascal, which handle routines such as input/output, screen commands and graphics. Often, books will introduce whole libraries at a time, usually a good way through the text. The approach of this book is different. If library routines exist to do the job, then they are used from the start.

The second type of unit used in this book is written by the authors. In order to help the reader to focus on the real problem solving aspects of the book, and to hide unnecessary detail until it can or should be explained, libraries are provided on the disk. In the early stages, you are asked to compile units without reading them, so that you need not be distracted by the actual Pascal code. The differences between different types of files are described in Chapter 2.

The third type of unit that you will be handling is written by yourself as the participating reader. The main programs described here require procedures that are specified within the book. In early case studies, these may be supplied ready-written on disk. In later case studies, the skeleton of such procedures may be provided on disk. This means that the framework of the procedure is supplied in a form that works, but does not carry out the full job as specified. Exercises set for the reader require you to adapt the code to do the job required. The advantage of supplying skeleton procedures is that they help you to avoid niggling early problems with the format of procedures or the language rules (syntax), as a version that compiles properly is provided. If you come across difficulties, then you can always revert to this version. Eventually, in later case studies, you will be specifying precisely what is needed in a library and writing it yourself.

The use of units from the start makes obvious the requirement to specify what a procedure does. This then makes the procedure the heart of the programming philosophy of this book, so you are being trained to think of programs in a modular as well as a 'top-down' way.

The disk that is supplied with this book is essential to studying with the book. It contains many files that are essential for the work that you will need to do. For each of the chapters from 3 to 10, there is some ready-written code. This is placed on the disk in the directory named with the chapter number. Each case study has been given a name. In Chapter 4, for example, the case study is called 'hotel'. A main program is provided as 'hotel.pas'. This uses procedures provided in libraries of ready-written code. In the case of the hotel, these files are named 'hotbase' and 'hotutil'.

Turbo Pascal would allow you to call the files anything you like, so long as the name does not clash with other existing names, and so long as it fits the Dos restriction to eight characters. In this book, a particular convention is used. The main programs will have three, four or five letter names, whichever is most suitable. Units will have names ending in 'base' or 'util', preceded by three or four letters of the main program to which they initially relate. This provides flexibility whilst making the file structure reasonable to follow.

Units used in this book are of two types. The 'util' units will normally be specially written to contain the procedures required by a particular program. (Because useful procedures that the program needs do not exist, they have to be invented.) The 'base' units will contain procedures, initially to be used by the corresponding 'util' unit, but which may later be used by several different programs or other units. In other words, they are those which may be 'recyclable'. In Chapter 4, for example, the files 'hotutil' and 'hotbase' are used. This approach of dividing procedure definitions into several files will come into its own in later case studies, but may initially seem a somewhat unnecessary distinction. When the case studies require data types and data structures to be defined, though, it should make obvious sense to define these in the 'base' unit so that they can be generally used.

It is not until Chapter 10, for example, that two 'base' units are used, namely logbase and hotbase, within the same case study. However, it is quite normal in somewhat earlier case studies to be using two or three system units and two or three user-written units.

Additionally, various exercises in the chapters of the book encourage you to develop a personalised library of commonly needed routines, such as a personalised welcome message and farewell message. These can then be incorporated into many of your subsequent programs. This file is referred to throughout as 'utils'.

How to work with the libraries

There is a lot of ready-written Pascal code which you will need to use whilst working through this book. This code is provided on the companion disk supplied with the book. You will need a disciplined approach to the management of the code provided and the code which you will be asked to write. This should ensure that you will maximise the enjoyment you gain from the book, and minimise the frustration from losing work on files.

The first practical task which you should carry out is to make a full copy of the disk provided. The disk provided should then be stored safely, as it may be needed in an emergency to recover code, but if all works to plan, it will not be needed at all.

On the disk, there are directories corresponding to each of the chapters in which you will be exploring the ready-written case studies. There are therefore directories on the disk called chap3, chap4, and so on, up to chap10. These each contain the code relevant to the work of a particular chapter.

An additional directory, utils, contains a version of the utility library which you should be developing in various chapters of the book. This is a simple version of utils. It is not as good as the imaginative version which you should be writing. It is only provided in case you wish to use it for later case studies without completing previous chapters. Such an approach is not an advisable one; readers will learn best by trying things out for themselves and persisting until they understand properly. The utility library solution is provided, however, so that continuation to later chapters is not too restricted if readers are failing to make progress.

Conclusion

This, then, is not a book to browse or dip in to. Ideas are tackled in a sequence with later ideas being very dependent on earlier ones. Dipping in and reading a chapter in isolation will be frustrating; the latest concept may depend on several introduced earlier. The latest code may depend on several earlier pieces of code.

Please do not dip into this book. Dive in! Join us in exploring the depth and power of programming, using Turbo Pascal as the medium. You will not be disappointed.

2
Using Turbo Pascal

This chapter is intended to get you started in Turbo Pascal. It covers enough Dos to enable you to copy the tutorial disk and load the Turbo environment. All the file and directory manipulation described here may be done quickly and easily in Windows, using the File Manager. Use of the Windows File Manager is not covered in this book. For most users, Turbo Pascal is still a Dos application, and therefore some familiarity with Dos will be of benefit. Readers already sufficiently familiar with Dos and/or Windows may therefore omit Section 2.2, and proceed directly from 2.1 to 2.3.

2.1   What is programming?

Programming involves using a computer to help solve problems. A computer is very good and fast at certain tasks, but it cannot think, and cannot solve a problem from a vague description of what needs to be done. The job of the programmer is to solve the problem by producing a set of instructions or an algorithm, and then to translate the algorithm into language that the computer can understand.

You will have come across algorithms in many situations. A cake recipe is an algorithm: it gives a set of instructions to be followed, but it does not actually bake the cake for you. Other algorithms include knitting patterns, music scores, and step-by-step instructions in car manuals. If the algorithm has been written correctly, it will allow you to solve the problem. By following the steps exactly, you can produce a mouth-watering cake, a well-fitting jumper, a recognisable tune or a road-worthy car.

One slight problem with computers is that they do not (yet) understand English. Their language is one of bits, of strings of ones and zeros. Writing algorithms or programs in machine code of ones and zeros is extremely tedious and prone to errors. High-level, or English-like, programming languages were developed in an attempt to overcome this problem. English itself is a very complex language, full of ambiguities and shades of meaning which can be interpreted intuitively by another English-speaking human, but would only cause confusion and errors for a machine. So programming languages like Pascal use only a small vocabulary and have very strict grammar rules, with every word precisely defined and no ambiguities. A special program called a compiler takes the English-like program and turns it into machine code which can be understood and executed by the computer.

In this book, you will learn how to write algorithms, how to turn them into programs in the Pascal language, and how to instruct the Pascal environment to compile them into machine code and then execute them.

2.2 A Dos introduction

It is assumed that you are using a version of Pascal designed to run under Dos, and that it is already installed on your hard disk. If it is not installed, you should install it now, following the installation instructions in the manual. If you are using a Windows version, then you may want to work entirely under Windows, and can therefore omit this section.

2.2.1 DRIVES AND DIRECTORIES

Your first task is to locate Turbo Pascal on the hard disk. The files needed to use Turbo Pascal will be collected together in a directory, which will probably be called 'turbo' or 'tp'. The hard disk on a stand-alone PC is usually known as the C drive. If you are using a network, Pascal may be on a drive with another letter. The exercise here assumes that you are working on a stand-alone PC with a hard drive called C.

EXERCISE 2.1

Check which drive you are on currently. The operating system prompt should be:

`C:\>`

which tells you that the operating system is ready for you to type in a command. If the prompt uses a different letter, e.g.

`A:\>`

then type

`C:      <Enter>`

to change to the C drive, where `<Enter>` means press the Enter or Return key.
If the `C:` is present, but there are other words between \ and > then type

`cd \     <Enter>`

to get back to the root directory.

The directories on your disk are arranged in a tree structure, somewhat similar to a family tree, but with the root at the top of the tree. A directory usually contains files, but may also contain other directories, which are then subdirectories of this main directory.

You can view the contents of the directory by using the Dos command 'dir'.

```
C:\> dir

 Volume in drive C is MS-DOS_6
 Volume Serial Number is 1CB1-22A0
 Directory of C:\
```

DOS	`<DIR>`	17/05/94	4:21
VALE	`<DIR>`	17/05/94	4:31
CLUTIL	`<DIR>`	24/05/94	2:21
MOUSE	`<DIR>`	24/05/94	2:21
WINDOWS	`<DIR>`	24/05/94	2:22
MARGARET	`<DIR>`	31/05/94	23:42
LOTUS	`<DIR>`	01/06/94	17:31

LSPRO2		\<DIR\>	01/06/94	21:34
GAMES		\<DIR\>	04/06/94	10:18
MISC		\<DIR\>	25/07/94	22:53
PROLOG		\<DIR\>	22/02/96	23:52
TEMP		\<DIR\>	04/01/95	23:21
PASCAL		\<DIR\>	23/07/95	21:55
COMMAND	COM	54,619	30/09/93	6:20
WINA20	386	9,349	13/02/94	6:21
CONFIG	SYS	333	08/01/96	10:55
AUTOEXEC	BAT	527	08/01/96	11:05

In this example, the root directory contains 17 items, of which 13 are subdirectories and four are files.

EXERCISE 2.2

List the root directory of your hard disk.
Identify the items which are subdirectories, and the items which are files.

The command 'cd' (change directory) allows you to move between directories. In the example above,

```
cd pascal
```

changes the operating system prompt to

```
C:\PASCAL>
```

and a directory listing (dir) now gives:

```
Volume in drive C is MS-DOS_6
Volume Serial Number is 1CB1-22A0
Directory of C:\PASCAL
```

.		\<DIR\>	23/07/95	21:56
..		\<DIR\>	23/07/95	21:56
TVISION		\<DIR\>	23/07/95	21:58
TVDEMOS		\<DIR\>	23/07/95	21:58
DOCDEMOS		\<DIR\>	23/07/95	21:58
DEMOS		\<DIR\>	23/07/95	21:58
DOC		\<DIR\>	23/07/95	21:58
BGI		\<DIR\>	23/07/95	21:58
UTILS		\<DIR\>	23/07/95	21:58
TURBO3		\<DIR\>	23/07/95	21:58
README	COM	4,217	23/10/90	6:00
UNZIP	EXE	23,044	23/10/90	6:00
TURBO	EXE	325,397	23/10/90	6:00
TURBO	TPL	45,344	23/10/90	6:00
TURBO	TP	2,183	23/07/95	22:00
TPC	EXE	69,214	23/10/90	6:00
TPTOUR	EXE	79,065	23/10/90	6:00
TPTOUR0	CBT	14,631	23/10/90	6:00
TPTOUR1	CBT	165,021	23/10/90	6:00
TPTOUR_P	CBT	8,327	23/10/90	6:00

TPTOUR_S	CBT	12,885	23/10/90	6:00
TPTOUR_U	CBT	11,489	23/10/90	6:00
README		16,417	23/10/90	6:00
TURBO	HLP	669,154	23/10/90	6:00
TPC	CFG	141	23/07/95	22:00

```
            25 file(s)           1,446,529 bytes
                               15,847,424 bytes free
```

EXERCISE 2.3

Locate the Turbo Pascal directory on your hard disk.
Change to that directory, and list the directory.
You should see a file called
TURBO.EXE
This is the program you need to run Turbo Pascal.

You will have noticed by now that Dos is not case sensitive. That is, it will accept commands in lower case, upper case, or a mixture of the two, and does not distinguish between upper case and lower case input. Dos will always respond in upper case.

If you need to create a new directory, this can be done with the command 'md' (for <u>m</u>ake <u>dir</u>ectory) followed by the required name. Dos names for files and directories are restricted to eight characters, plus up to three characters for an extension. So if you wanted to create a new subdirectory of the pascal directory, and call it work, then first you should make sure that you are in the directory pascal, as this is to be the parent directory of work:

```
C:\PASCAL> md work
```

If the command is correct, the computer will not respond with a message, it will merely repeat the prompt. But if you type 'dir' or 'cd work' , you will see that the new directory has indeed been created.

Directories can be removed by the command

```
rd <directory name>   (for remove directory).
```

A directory should only be removed if it is empty. Dos will give a message if the directory is not empty and still contains some files. These files will need to be deleted or moved elsewhere before the directory is removed.

2.2.2   FILES

There will be times when you need to make a copy of a file. You will need to make backup copies of important files, and you may also want to make a copy of a file before you start altering it. That way, if anything goes wrong with the amended version, you can always return to the original and start again. You will also find it useful to copy the latest version of your utils.pas file into the appropriate directory whenever you start a new case study. The Dos command for copying a file is

```
copy <source> <destination>
```

So, for example, if you want to copy your utils.pas file from the chap3 directory to the chap4 directory on your floppy disk, you could type:

```
copy a:\chap3\utils.pas a:\chap4\utils.pas
```

and if you wanted to copy bank.pas from the chap8 directory on your floppy disk to the tp\work directory on the C drive, renaming the file bank2.pas, you could type:

```
copy a:\chap8\bank.pas c:\tp\work\bank2.pas
```

There are various abbreviations that you can use when specifying filenames, details of which can be found in any Dos manual.

Files can be deleted by the del <filename> command. If the file is in the current directory, you only need to specify the filename. If the file is in a different directory, you will need to specify more of the pathname. The pathname is the full name which specifies the drive and the path taken from the root directory to reach a particular file or directory. So

```
C:\TP\WORK> del bank2.pas
```

would be sufficient to delete bank2.pas from the current directory. But

```
A:\CHAP8> del c:\tp\work\bank2.pas
```

would be required to delete the same file if the current directory were chap8 on the A drive.

Filenames consist of two parts. The main name of the file can be up to eight characters, but an extension of up to three characters is also allowed. The extension is used to signify the type of file, for example, Pascal program files have an extension .pas, while word processed files often have an extension .doc, and clipart may have an extension .wmf or .pcx. The extension .exe is used for executable files, such as games, the Pascal environment, and the compiled versions of the programs you will be writing. An exe file can be run independently of the programming environment that created it, and is run by just typing its name.

2.2.3   WILDCARDS

Wildcards allow groups of files to be specified in the same command. Dos allows the use of two wildcards:

   ? to replace exactly 1 character, and
   * to replace 0 or more characters.

So, for example,

```
dir t*.exe
```

would give a directory listing of all the files in that directory beginning with t and with the extension .exe. The listing could include t.exe, turbo.exe and tpc.exe, but not turbo.hlp or unzip.exe.

```
del prog?.pas
```

would delete all the files in the directory with a five-letter name beginning 'prog', and a .pas extension. So prog1.pas and prog9.pas would be deleted, but not myprog.pas, prog10.pas, or prog1.doc.

2.2.4   COPYING DISKS

It is possible, but tedious, to copy a disk one file at a time. It is much quicker to use a diskcopy command. Use the command 'diskcopy' itself to make a complete copy of a floppy disk to another floppy disk of identical type. So to make a working copy of the disk that came with this book, on to another disk of the same size and capacity, type:

```
diskcopy a: a: or diskcopy a: b:
```

according to whether you have a single (A:) or double (A: and B:) floppy drive. You will be prompted to insert the correct disk at the appropriate time. You are strongly advised to write-protect your source disk whenever performing a diskcopy. Then if you do accidentally insert the source disk instead of the destination disk, you will not lose all your data. Write-protect the disk by moving the little plastic square in the top left corner on the back of the disk, so that the hole is open.

Diskcopy cannot be used to transfer files to or from a hard disk, or between floppy disks of different sizes or capacities. In these cases, use the command 'xcopy'. Xcopy can be used to copy specified files or groups of files, and wildcards can be used. Unlike copy, which only copies files, xcopy will copy subdirectories too, preserving the directory structure.

So, to copy the contents of a floppy disk, including all the subdirectories, to a directory called work on the hard disk, type:

```
xcopy a:\*.* c:\work
```

2.3   The tutorial disk

The tutorial disk supplied with this book is essential. Without it, you will not be able to complete the case studies described in Chapters 3–10. Your first task, therefore, is to make a copy of the original disk. If you believe in a 'belt and braces' approach to life, then make two copies, as you will be working on and altering the first copy. Ensure the original disk is write-protected, and then perform a diskcopy or an xcopy as described above, or copy the disk using the File Manager in Windows. Put the original disk away somewhere safely, in case you need to retrieve files from it again at a later date.

Success in programming relies in part on good housekeeping. The tutorial disk is already set up with a directory for each chapter which contains a case study. You are strongly recommended to keep to this system, and to create new directories as you need them for the later chapters. Weed your disk at intervals, to remove temporary files that you created while experimenting, and no longer need. A comment and date at the start of each file and amended program may save you hours of searching later. Above all, resist the temptation to dump everything into one huge directory, just to save copying a file or two between directories. The old saying 'Lazy people take most pains' is as true of program file organisation as it is of any other area of organisation.

2.4   The Turbo Pascal environment

This section introduces the Borland Turbo Pascal environment. With each upgrade to Pascal, more features have been added to the environment. Earlier versions did not recognise the existence of a mouse, while later versions allow the user to use mouse or keyboard or both, the keyboard commands remaining unchanged. The subset of commands and features given here is enough to allow you to load, edit and save files, to compile units and programs, and to build and run completed programs. Where necessary, specific instructions are given for versions 4 and 6, as these still seem to be the versions of Turbo Pascal most widely available in schools and colleges. The vast majority of the commands can be used unchanged in versions 5 or 7. For more information, you should consult your Borland Turbo Pascal manual, or the Turbo Pascal on-line help.

Turbo Pascal is supplied with an integrated development environment, which means that you can load and save files, and edit, compile and run programs without ever leaving Turbo Pascal. To load the environment you need to change directory to the Turbo Pascal directory, and then run the program turbo.exe. You do this by simply typing

```
turbo
```

whereupon the main screen should appear as shown in Figure. 2.1.

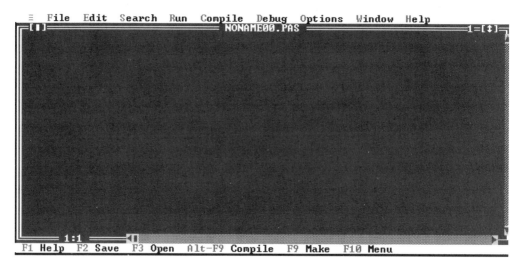

Figure 2.1 Turbo Pascal main screen

The screen is divided into three sections. The top line is the menu bar, a main menu with pull-down submenus. The bottom line gives a quick reference to the F keys and their current functions. From version 6, in addition to the keys listed:

- pressing F6 allows you to move between any open files, including the Pascal clipboard;
- pressing Alt + F5 allows you to toggle between the edit window and the output screen (where the '+' sign is used to indicate that you should hold down the Alt key while pressing the F5 key).

Within a menu, you can:

- highlight a menu name using cursor keys or the mouse, and then select it by pressing <Enter> or clicking the left mouse button;
- press <escape> to leave the menu;
- press F1 for context-sensitive help, or Ctrl + F1 for general help;
- press F10 to return to the main menu;
- press ALT + (F,E,R,C,O, etc.) to invoke the command with that initial letter from the main menu;
- press ALT + X to quit to Dos.

On exit, you will be prompted to save any files which have been altered since they were last saved.

2.5 The File menu

The File pull-down menu is shown in Figure 2.2.

It is used to load, create, print (not in Version 4) and save files and also to quit from the Turbo Pascal environment. You should use the 'Change dir' command every time you load Pascal, to ensure that files are loaded and saved from and to the correct directory on your tutorial disk. This is particularly important when you are compiling units, to ensure that the compiled code produced is placed in the correct directory, from which it will be accessed later.

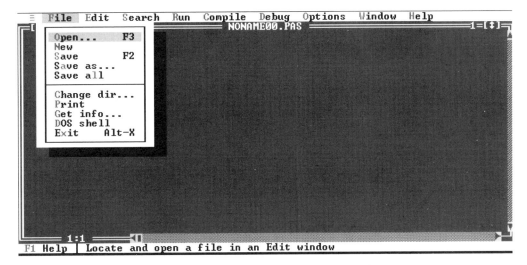

Figure 2.2 The Turbo Pascal File menu

2.6   The Compile menu

Figure 2.3 shows the Compile pull-down menu.

```
≡   File   Edit   Search   Run   Compile   Debug   Options   Window   Help
┌[■]══════════════════════════════════════════════════════════════1=[‡]┐
│PROGRAM message1;         ┌──────────────────────────┐                 ▲
│                          │ Compile      Alt-F9       │                 ■
│<                         │ Make           F9         │
│   Main program for Chapte│ Build                     │
│   displays a message at t│ Destination   Memory      │tred,  in the
│   required colour and wit│ Primary file...           │
│   Written by AMC/MPW      └──────────────────────────┘
│   1:1:96
│>
│
│USES messbase, utils, crt;
│
│VAR message : STRING;
│    colour  : INTEGER;
│
│BEGIN
│     GetMessage(message, colour);
│     TextColor(colour);
│     TextBackground(Black);
│     ClrScr;
│     DisplayMessage(message);                                          ▼
├───── 1:1 ═════◄▮►══════════════════════════════════════════════════►┤
│ F1 Help │ Compile source file
```

Figure 2.3 The Turbo Pascal Compile menu

Change the Destination option to Disk rather than Memory to ensure that compiled files are stored permanently on disk and not temporarily stored in memory. The option is toggled (switched) between the two options using the <Enter> key.

Use Compile if you want to compile the single file currently in the editor. Make and Build are alternatives when compiling program files. Build will compile the program and also all the library files associated with it. Make will only recompile those library files whose source code has changed since they were last compiled.

2.7 The Run menu

The Run command will perform a Make if the program file currently being edited has changed since it was last compiled, and then Run the program.

2.8 The editor

The Turbo Pascal editor is very similar to the Wordstar word processor. There are about 50 keyboard commands which can be used to move the cursor, mark out and move text, and so on. The most useful commands are summarised below.

Movement commands

Character left	left arrow
Character right	right arrow
Line up	up arrow
Line down	down arrow
Page up	Page Up
Page down	Page Down
Beginning of file	Ctrl + Page Up
End of file	Ctrl + Page Down

(where again, '+' is used to show that the first key should be held down while pressing the second).

Insert and delete commands

Insert/overwrite toggle	Ins
Insert line	Ctrl + N
Delete line	Ctrl + Y

Block commands

Mark start of block at current cursor position	Ctrl + K, B (i.e. press Ctrl + K, and then B) (Note that the block is not highlighted until the end is marked)
Mark end of block at current cursor position	Ctrl + K, K
Move marked block to current cursor position	Ctrl + K, V
Copy marked block to current cursor position	Ctrl + K, C
Delete marked block	Ctrl + K, Y

(Note that highlighting can be removed by pressing Ctrl + K, B followed by Ctrl + K, K at the same point.)

Miscellaneous commands

Autoindent on/off	Ctrl + O, I
Tabs available on/off	Ctrl + O, T
Find and replace	Ctrl + Q, A

The block highlighting commands and cursor movement can also be performed using the mouse.

Cut and paste and copy and paste may also be performed using the mouse and the Edit menu. If more than one file is open, cut or copy and paste between files may also be performed, using the

Turbo Pascal clipboard. This facility is not available in Version 4, which only allows one file at a time to be open.

2.9   The other menu options

A detailed examination of the other options on the main menu is beyond the scope of this brief introduction. They are there to be explored, and you are encouraged to do this. In particular, the on-line Help provision has improved with each new release of Turbo Pascal.

2.10   Printing files

There are several ways of printing a Pascal file, some of which are described below. For Version 6, the simplest method is to print directly using the Print option on the File menu. You can also print directly from the Pascal environment in Version 4 by using Write To . . . from the file menu. First, save the program in the normal way, then Write to . . . prn, and then reload the file with its original name as soon as it has been printed.

Pascal files are in ASCII text format. To print your file, therefore, you can print straight from Dos using the command:

```
type myprog.pas >prn
```

where >prn redirects the listing from the screen to the printer.

Alternatively, you can load your program as a text file into any word processor package, and print from there. Later, when you write much longer programs, you may even prefer to code your program in a word processing environment and then export it as a text file for use within the Pascal environment.

2.11   Naming files

The convention used in this book for naming files within a case study has already been mentioned in Chapter 1. In addition, Pascal has some naming conventions for the three-letter extension in the file name:

Pascal source code files for both programs and units have the extension	.pas
Compiled (library) units have the extension	.tpu
Executable files (compiled programs) have the extension	.exe

.exe files can be run from Dos, independently of the Pascal environment.

EXERCISE 2.4

The description of the Turbo Pascal environment above was written primarily for Version 6. You should ensure that you can do the following tasks in whichever version of Turbo Pascal you are using.

Step 1. Load the Pascal environment with a new file. Using the editor as a simple word processor, write a paragraph about yourself and what you hope to achieve by working through this book. Ensure that you can save the file to disk, print it, and retrieve it again next time you load Pascal.

Step 2. Load the file chap2\editor.pas from your tutorial disk. It provides an exercise in using the editor. Read the file and follow the instructions for editing it.

3
Messages

After tackling this chapter you should understand:

- the use of the Turbo Pascal environment to edit, compile and run a program
- how to load, save and print files
- how to test a program
- how to produce an algorithm for solving a simple problem
- the following Pascal concepts:
  - program header
  - comments
  - how to use a library (unit)
  - variables of type integer and string
  - begin and end
  - procedures with parameters.

After tackling this chapter you will have produced a utilities unit containing the following procedures:

- Welcome
- Farewell
- Pause
- RestoreColour.

3.1   Introduction to message

In this chapter, you will work on a program which will display a message on the screen. The user will enter the message from the keyboard, together with instructions about where on the screen, and in which colour, the message is to be displayed. The problem can be broken down into three questions to ask the user:

1. What message do you want to display?
2. Where on the screen do you want the message to be displayed?
3. What colour do you want?

The first question is very straightforward, but the second and third questions may invite further questions. For example, the user may respond to the third question by asking 'Do you mean the colour of the text, or the colour of the background?' The second question invites even more complications:

'Can I decide exactly where I want the message to start?';
'Do I have to tell you how long the message is?';
'Do you need to know where it is going to end?';
'How big is the screen?';
'Can't I just have the message in the centre of the screen?'

As a programmer, you need to be able to anticipate all the questions and ambiguities which lie behind what looks at first like a very simple problem. You need to decide exactly what the program will, or will not do, what input the program will require from the user, and what the output is going to be. Often this will involve setting boundaries on an open-ended problem.

Whatever you eventually decide about the display, your program must contain two steps:

1. Accept data from the user.
2. Display information on the screen.

This is a simple version of a common pattern in programming. Many problems and programs consist of three overall steps:

1. Enter the data.
2. Process the data, turning it into information.
3. Output the information.

The idea of data processing is that raw data is gathered and input to the computer. There it is processed, and turned from a collection of seemingly jumbled and unrelated words and numbers into meaningful information which can be put to good use. In this particular case, the processing element is minimal.

One approach to programming then takes each step and considers what needs to be done, specifying the task in more detail. In this case, the first step can be further specified as:

1. Accept data from the user.
    (a) Accept a message.
    (b) Accept a position instruction.
    (c) Accept a colour instruction.

The 'position instruction' of step 1(b) above can then be further expanded, into more detail, depending on what the user wants, what the programmer would like to offer, and what is feasible.

This method of breaking the problem down into its simpler components is called 'top-down design'. The solution is implemented as a structured program, in which each level uses a number of the building blocks produced in the levels below. In Pascal, these building blocks are called procedures and functions. The procedures and functions are collected together into one or more units.

3.2 A simple display program

EXERCISE 3.1

A programmer has decided on a solution, and written a program to display messages.
You will find the program as message1.exe in the directory chap3 on your tutorial disk.

Step 1. Insert the tutorial disk into your disk drive, and run the program by typing

`a:\chap3\message1`

Step 2. Try running the program several times, following the instructions on the screen, and using different messages and different colours.

Step 3. Write down what the program actually does. Is this what you would want under all circumstances?

You should have found that the user is asked for the message, and for the colour required. You had to input a number for the colour, but could only find by trial and error which number corresponded to the different colours available – not a very user-friendly feature of the program. (Did you try number 0? If not, try it now.)

The message always appeared in the centre of the top line of the screen. (Did you test what happened if you input a message too long for one line? If not, try it now. What is the longest message you are allowed?)

Finally, you needed to press the 'enter' key in order to leave the program. This may not have been obvious.

Did you write down the messages and colours you used, or did you just try to remember them? Testing a program is a very important part of programming, and needs to be done carefully and methodically – although it may seem easier just to test a program randomly, it makes more work in the long run. Testing will be covered in detail in the next chapter, but for this program record your testing and results in a simple table such as:

Message	Colour	Result
Hello World	14	Hello World at top centre of screen, in yellow
Today is Friday	0	Blank screen

The program message1 appears below:

```
PROGRAM message1;
{
   Main program for Chapter 3 - Messages
   Displays a message at the top of the screen, centred, in the
   required colour and with a black background
   Written by AMC/MPW
   1:1:96
}
USES messbase, utils, crt;

VAR message : STRING;
    colour  : INTEGER;

BEGIN
   GetMessage(message, colour);
   TextColor(colour);
   TextBackground(Black);
   ClrScr;
```

```
    DisplayMessage(message);
    RestoreColour
END.  {message1}
```

In this book, Pascal keywords will always be written in upper case (capital letters) in program listings. This convention makes programs easier to read, and easier to debug when they contain errors. However, lower case will be used in the main text for ease of reading. Quotation marks will be used around such words when necessary in order to emphasise them.

The program is in two parts, the declarations and the action. The declarations tell the compiler about the various things you, the programmer, want to use in the program, and the names, or 'identifiers', you have given them. The action part is bracketed between 'begin' and 'end', and is the set of instructions to be carried out when the program is run.

Look first at the declarations. The first line is called the program header, and tells the compiler what you have decided to call your program. It is not essential to give the program a name; you could omit this line altogether. But it is good practice to include it, and you are recommended to give the same name to the program and to the file which contains it. So the program message1 can be found in the disk file message1.pas.

The next line starts with an opening brace { , and you will see a closing brace } several lines further down. Anything enclosed in braces is ignored by the compiler; it is written for the human reader, and called a comment. Comments are very useful; they remind you what a program, or part of a program, does. When you look at a program after an interval of six months, you are unlikely to remember much about it, so comments are very useful memory joggers. If someone else has to alter your program in your absence, the task will be much easier if you have carefully documented what the program does – and where better to document a program than within it? The comments should also indicate who wrote the program, and when. Remember to change the date every time you change the code. Always write the comments as you write the program. It is the only way to ensure they actually are written. If you leave them until the program is otherwise finished, it is easy to omit them altogether, claiming shortage of time. This is often a false economy in time, as an uncommented program is so much more difficult to read than a well-documented one.

The next line, which begins 'uses ...' tells the compiler which units, or library files, to look in to find various items that will be needed later in the program. These items may be needed for either the declaration or the action section. Not everything has to be defined in a unit, as Pascal provides basic variable types, such as numbers and letters, and procedures for input and output. Because they are available everywhere in any Pascal program or library, these are known as pervasive types and procedures. This program uses three units or library files, messbase.pas and utils.pas are units written specially for this case study. Crt is a unit supplied with Turbo Pascal, and contains a number of useful procedures for handling the screen display, such as changing colours of text or background, clearing the screen, and moving the cursor. Notice that the units in the list are separated by commas. In Pascal, items in lists are usually separated by commas.

Punctuation is very important in programming, and a program will not compile unless the correct punctuation is used throughout. A number of punctuation symbols are used in Pascal, and each must be used correctly. As stated above, the comma is used to separate items in a list. The semicolon is used to separate declarations in the declaration section of a program, and to separate statements in the action section of a program. The table below shows the main punctuation used in Pascal. Some of the items in the table will not be encountered until much later in the book, but they are included here for completeness.

Punctuation symbol	Name	Use in Pascal programs
,	comma	to separate items in a list
;	semicolon	to separate declarations and statements
:	colon	to separate a list of identifiers from their type in a declaration
' '	single quotation marks	to denote a literal char or string
.	full stop or period or dot	to terminate a program to separate a record name qualifier from a field name
..	two dots	to show the lower and upper bounds of a subrange
( )	parentheses or round brackets	to enclose arithmetic and logical expressions to enclose the parameter list in a procedure or function
[ ]	square brackets	to enclose a subrange in an array declaration to enclose an array index to enclose a list of set members
{ }	braces or curly brackets	to enclose comments

The final line of the declaration section tells the compiler to reserve some storage space for the variables you are going to use. The variable declarations always start with the word 'var'. You are going to use two variables. One of them is going to be called message, and is going to contain some text, which Pascal calls a 'string'. The other will be called colour, and is declared as an 'integer' type, which means a whole number. The rules of Pascal grammar state that identifiers (that is, names of variables, procedures, programs, etc.) must always start with a letter, and may contain any combination of letters and digits plus a few other characters such as the underscore. Spaces are not allowed in identifiers, so the underscore or initial capitals should be used when necessary to aid readability (e.g. my_col, GetMessage). Identifiers should always be meaningful, as it is much easier to read a program written in terms of meaningful words such as message, colour, length, etc. than if the variables are called a, b, c, d, ... just in the order they happen to be used or in the order in which they were thought of by the programmer. Every variable must be declared before it can be used, so that the Pascal compiler can reserve the correct amount of storage space for it. Note that the variable name and its type are always separated by a colon (:), and that the variable declarations are separated from each other by a semicolon (;). In this program, there are only two variables to be declared, and they are of different types. If there are several variables of the same type, they can be declared as a list separated by commas, for example:

```
VAR   length, width, height : INTEGER;
      remark, sentence       : STRING;
```

The six lines bracketed between 'begin' and 'end' are the action of the program. They are a set of calls to six procedures which the compiler will find by looking in the three units listed in the 'uses ...' line. Note that the procedure calls are separated by semicolons. The action part of a program consists of

```
BEGIN
     { statements separated by semicolons }
END.
```

Semicolons are required to separate the statements, but not to separate the components of the overall 'begin–statements–end' structure. Therefore, no semicolon is required after 'begin' or before 'end'.

Three of the procedures used are supplied with Turbo Pascal, and can be found in the unit crt. These are TextColor, TextBackground, and ClrScr.

ClrScr – clears the screen of any text.
TextBackground – changes the background colour to the value in brackets.
TextColor – changes the text colour to the value in brackets.

Note the spelling of 'TextColor'. Turbo Pascal is an American product, so the procedures provided by Pascal use American spelling. The program message1 was written on the other side of the Atlantic, so uses English spelling for such identifiers as 'colour'. The compiler will accept either spelling for the declaration of an identifier, but once an identifier has been declared, exactly the same spelling must be used whenever it is referenced.

The values in brackets are called parameters. The parameters provide the specific data or information on which the procedure will act.

ClrScr does not need any parameters, since it just clears whatever is on the screen.

TextColor and TextBackground each need one parameter, the required colour. The colour can be given in the program either as its name, from a list of valid colours, e.g. Yellow, or as a number code, e.g. 14. The list of colour names and their corresponding number codes is held in crt. In this program, the parameter for TextBackground is always the same, Black. The parameter for TextColor is a variable, colour, and its value will depend on the value you choose to enter when prompted for a colour code number. The way the program is written at the moment means that you have to enter a number for the colour code; you cannot enter a colour name directly from the keyboard. The colour names, such as Black, Yellow, Green, are an example of an enumerated type. The use of enumerated types in a program aids readability; the compiler translates values into numbers, so TextColor(Yellow) will be translated into TextColor(14). They will be covered in more detail in a later chapter. The full list of text and background colours available is given in Appendix 1.

The other three procedures were written for this case study and are found in the units messbase and utils. Units are also known more generally as libraries, although 'unit' is the specific Turbo Pascal word for such files. Messbase contains the two procedures GetMessage and DisplayMessage, both of which have parameters. GetMessage has two parameters; one to hold the message, and the other to hold the required colour code number. DisplayMessage only needs one parameter, the message itself, as the colours have been set already by the procedure calls in the previous two lines. Finally, there is a call to RestoreColour. This is a procedure in utils, which restores the screen to white text on a black background.

Like Dos, Pascal is not case sensitive; this means that the compiler will recognise begin, BEGIN, Begin, and even bEgIn as all being the same word. However, consistent use of upper and lower case letters aids readability of programs. In this book, the following conventions are used:

• Pascal reserved words and predefined types are always written in upper case letters, e.g. BEGIN and INTEGER;

- procedure and function names always begin with a capital letter, and each word has an initial capital if the identifier consists of more than one word, e.g. DisplayMessage; remember that spaces are not allowed in identifiers;
- variable names are entirely in lower case, unless the identifier consists of more than one word and use of a capital letter makes it much easier to read, e.g. mycolour or myColour.

EXERCISE 3.2

Step 1. Load Turbo Pascal and then load the file message1.pas from the directory chap3 on your tutorial disk. You will see that it contains the Pascal program message1 described earlier.

Step 2. In order to compile the program, you will first need to load the units messbase and utils and compile them. Ensure that you compile to disk and not memory, and that the compiled (.tpu) files are saved in the chap3 directory. Do not worry about the contents of these units at this stage; they will be examined in detail later.

Step 3. Now reload message1, compile and run it.
(Hint: If you get an error message such as 'Cannot find messbase.tpu' check in the file menu that you have changed directory to a:\chap3.)

Step 4. Use the editor to remove the line RestoreColour, compile and run again. Is there any difference?

Step 5. Now run the program again. What happens this time?

RestoreColour ensures that everything is returned to 'normal' at the end of the program. Utility procedures like this are very useful, and worth collecting together into a library. You will start to do this later in the chapter.

Programming languages have a small vocabulary and very strict grammar or syntax. If you make a spelling mistake in English, or use a colon where you really should have used a full stop, it often does not really matter, because humans are very good at sensing the intended meaning. But a misplaced comma in a Pascal program will mean the compiler registers an error and compilation halts. Similarly, if a word is spelled wrong, a human can make an intelligent guess at the intended word. But the compiler will not recognise it.

EXERCISE 3.3

Step 1. Reload the original version of message1.pas from your tutorial disk.

Step 2. Experiment by introducing errors, one at a time, into the program, such as spelling and punctuation errors, or removing words from the declaration section. Try using the wrong parameter in a procedure call, or adding an extra parameter. Record what you did, and the error message obtained each time when you tried to compile the program. Try to interpret the error messages.

Some of the errors you introduced were compiler errors. Compiler errors are errors in the syntax of the program, such as spelling or punctuation errors. Until all the compiler errors have been corrected, the program cannot be compiled and so cannot run.

Compiler errors are not the only type of error in programs. Sometimes a program fails while it is running, due to a run-time or execution error. Common run-time errors include a user attempting to enter letters when the program is expecting numbers, or an attempt to divide by zero.

A third type of program error is the logic error, and this can be very hard to discover. A program compiles and runs without error, but it does not give 'the right answers'. Perhaps you mistyped a formula, or squared a number when you should have taken the square root, or started searching a list of names from part way through it instead of from the beginning. A good test plan, where you use data for which you know the answer in advance, will help to eliminate this type of error.

3.3 Improving the solution

Make a list of improvements that could be made to the program. How could it be made more generally useful, or more user friendly?

You are now going to alter the program to allow the user to choose the background colour as well as the text colour. A list of valid colours and colour codes is given in Appendix 1.

EXERCISE 3.4

Step 1. Load message1.pas.

Step 2. Use the Save As . . . or Write To . . . command in the File menu to save a new copy of the file with the name message2.pas. You will now work on this version of the program.

Step 3. Use the editor to change the program name to message2, to alter the date and to add 'amended by <your name>' to the programmers' names. Also, alter the comment after the final 'end.' to the name of the new program.

Step 4. Instead of GetMessage, you will need to use the procedure GetInput, which is also in messbase. GetInput has three parameters, to hold the message, the text colour, and the background colour. So replace the GetMessage line by:

```
GetInput(message, textcol, backcol);
```

Step 5. You will need to tell the compiler about the two new variables you are using, and you no longer need to declare colour, as it is not going to be used. So change the variable declaration to

```
VAR message          : STRING;
    textcol, backcol : INTEGER;
```

Alternatively, the second variable declaration could be written in longer form as

```
   textcol : INTEGER;
   backcol : INTEGER;
```

Step 6. Now change the parameters in the calls to TextColor and TextBackground so that they use the new information.

Step 7. Finally, change the comment at the top of the program to reflect what the amended program now does.

Step 8. Save your program, compile and run. You do not have to recompile the units, as they have not changed.

If you have any difficulty, compare your solution with message3.pas on the tutorial disk.

3.4   Writing to the screen

Pascal provides predefined, or pervasive, procedures for input and output. These are

Read and ReadLn for input, and
Write and WriteLn for output.

For keyboard input you should always use ReadLn. This ensures that the entire line is read, including the end of line character generated when you press the 'Enter' key. The end of line character is not normally required as part of the data, and so will be discarded.

For screen output, you may use either Write or WriteLn. The difference between them is that a call to WriteLn includes a carriage return (newline) after the required output is displayed. There is no newline after a call to Write, and the screen cursor remains at the next space after the end of the output.

Usually, ReadLn and WriteLn have one or more parameters. But they may also be used without parameters. ReadLn with no parameters is used to read and ignore anything that has been entered at the keyboard until the 'Enter' code is encountered. WriteLn with no parameters just moves the screen cursor to the start of the next line, without displaying anything else.

Output may be in one of two forms – a literal, or the contents of a memory location (a variable). For example, you may wish to display the word 'Hello' on the screen, or display a number which is stored as a variable called Hello. Pascal distinguishes between literals and variable names (identifiers) by enclosing literals in single quotes. Thus,

```
WriteLn('Hello');
```

will output the word Hello on the screen, as the parameter to the WriteLn procedure is a literal; whereas

```
WriteLn(Hello);
```

will display the contents of the variable Hello on the screen.

3.5   Personalising your programs

Commercial software usually has a Welcome screen, which is displayed as soon as the program is loaded. There may also be a Farewell screen, displayed when you exit from the program. In this exercise, you will create your own Welcome and Farewell screens, which can be added to any program you write from now on. As you learn more about programming, or when you tire of the flashing and clashing colours you initially choose for your messages, you can alter these screens as you wish. An important feature of structured, modular programs is that you can change one procedure without it having an effect on anything else in the program.

As has already been mentioned, you will be putting useful procedures into the unit utils.pas. So far, you have used RestoreColour from it. It also contains Welcome, Farewell and Pause procedures. If you look at the unit utils.pas, you will see that it contains two sections – the interface section and the implementation section, and that procedures are first listed in the interface and then repeated in the same order in the implementation. The interface section is used to describe what the procedures do, and is meant to be read by a programmer who just wants to use existing procedures. The implementation section contains the actual code; it describes how the action of the procedure is to be performed. The structure and syntax of procedures and units will be described in detail in later chapters. The code in the implementation section for the Welcome and Farewell procedures is currently as shown below:

```
PROCEDURE Welcome;

BEGIN
    ClrScr;
    WriteLn('Welcome to my program');
    GotoXY(1,25);
    Pause
END;   {Welcome}

PROCEDURE Farewell;

BEGIN
    ClrScr;
    WriteLn('Thank you for using my program');
    GotoXY(1,25);
    Pause
END;   {Farewell}
```

As you can see, the structure of a procedure declaration is very similar to that of a program. You are going to replace the WriteLn statement in each of these two procedures with your personalised message.

Two other procedures are also called. First, a call is made to GotoXY, in which two parameters are specified. This procedure is in the library unit crt supplied with Turbo Pascal, and allows the cursor to be placed anywhere on the screen. The coordinate of the top left corner of the text screen is (1,1) and the bottom right corner is (80,25), corresponding to 80 character positions on each of 25 lines on the screen. So GotoXY(1,25) positions the cursor in the bottom left corner, ready to display the message on the bottom line.

The final procedure call is to Pause, which is a pre-written procedure provided in utils. The implementation code for Pause is given below:

```
PROCEDURE Pause;

BEGIN
    Write('Press ENTER to continue');
    ReadLn;
    ClrScr
END; {Pause}
```

Pause also contains procedure calls. Firstly, a message is output to the screen. Then the procedure ReadLn is called. This effectively produces a pause – nothing else will happen until the user presses the 'Enter' key. Finally, there is a call to ClrScr, which is also found in crt, and causes the screen to be cleared.

Like RestoreColour, Pause is complete and ready to be used without further modification. As a user of the utils unit, you only need to read the interface entries for RestoreColour and Pause in order to see how to use them. You do not need to look at the implementation code as you are not going to alter it. However, you may like to look out of interest, to see how such procedures are written.

EXERCISE 3.5

Step 1. Load message1.pas from your tutorial disk.

Step 2. Alter the program so that it calls the Welcome procedure at the beginning, immediately after 'begin', and then calls the Farewell procedure at the end, immediately before 'end'.

Step 3. Compile and run the program, and save it as message4.pas.

The next task is to personalise the Welcome and Farewell messages, to make them your own. The existing procedures are known as skeleton procedures; the bare bones of the procedures are there, so they can be compiled and tested at an early stage of program writing, and then fleshed out later on. Skeleton procedures will be encountered again in later chapters.

EXERCISE 3.6

Step 1. Load utils.pas from your tutorial disk.

Step 2. Find the procedures Welcome and Farewell in the implementation section of the unit. Alter the WriteLn statements to give your own welcome and farewell messages to users of your programs.

Step 3. Compile and save utils.pas.

Step 4. Load message4.pas, compile and run it.
(Hint: if the display still uses the skeleton Welcome and Farewell procedures, check that you have set the compiler option to compile to disk, and not to memory, reload and recompile utils.pas, and try again.)

Step 5. Experiment in Welcome and Farewell with different colours, and different positions on the screen for your message, by calling the procedures TextColor, TextBackground and GotoXY with different values for the parameters.
(Hint: if you want to return to normal colours for the rest of the program, call RestoreColour just before END in procedure Welcome.)

EXERCISE 3.7

These exercises are designed to help you to test yourself on the knowledge which you should have acquired in reading this chapter and doing the previous exercises.

1. Explain the difference between a unit and a program.
2. Explain the difference between a system unit and a user-written unit, giving examples from this chapter.
3. Explain what is meant by 'pervasive'.
4. Explain in your own words the four input and output procedures described in this chapter.

5. Explain which items of a program appear in the declaration section and which in the action section.
6. Why is indentation used in programs?
7. How is a program told which units it is to use?
8. What is meant by a 'type'?
9. Express in your own words the rules governing Pascal identifiers.
10. Distinguish between compiler errors and other programming errors.

4
The hotel

Before starting this chapter you should be able to do the following:

- edit Pascal code in the Turbo Pascal environment
- compile units and programs
- run a program.

Before tackling this chapter you should have produced a utilities unit containing:

- Welcome
- Farewell
- Pause
- RestoreColour.

After tackling this chapter you should understand:

- the purpose and use of a test plan for a program
- the use of pre- and post-conditions and action statements of a procedure in order to make use of it
- the importance of the order of compilation of units and the use of unit dependency diagrams for describing this.

4.1   Introduction to hotel bookings

The main program in this chapter uses four units that together provide the elements of a solution to a simple hotel booking problem. These units, which are described below, will be used and amended by you. This will allow you to start with a working solution and then make improvements.

The program requirements are stated as follows.

Provide a program that a hotel could use for room bookings, where each room, numbered from 1 upwards, can be booked. The dialogue will allow the user to book a room by entering its number, and to enquire whether a particular room number is booked. A message should be displayed if an attempt is made to book a room that is already booked.

Having read the program requirements carefully, the first step is usually to decide the limitations that a programmer might place on this general description. This enables the solution to be much more definite. A professional programmer would respond to the person commissioning the work with a list of limitations. This enables the customer to be clear from the start about the detailed solution.

Working from the specification, it is suggested that the following boundaries are set down.

The program will hold information for one day only, and all information will be lost when the program is terminated. The program will allow for rooms numbered 1 to 20. The program will be menu-driven, and after entering the code that requests the termination of the program, a room number will still have to be entered, but this will be ignored.

These limitations might seem unusual and are unrealistic for a real hotel, but bear in mind that they arise out of the desire to make this a simple case study.

The holding of information for one day only is obviously an over-simplification and is not realistic, but this has been done to keep data handling and validation simple. You will not, at this stage, be examining how the data is held. You will be using ready-written routines that will allow you to interrogate the data and to change it.

The idea that data is lost when the program halts is also very unrealistic. This is done here, and in a number of later case studies, as file handling (that is the recording of data on disk for storing between runs) is not covered until Chapter 10. This is largely because the arrangement is straightforward, but the manipulation of files makes testing of programs more complicated. With the current arrangement, testing of the program can be based on the assurance that each time the program is run, the data starts in the same state.

The choice of 20 rooms is entirely arbitrary; any other number (within reason) could have been chosen. Later case studies will show how easy to alter such a limit can be. It is important, though, to make this choice clear to the person commissioning the program from the start. If the choice of 20 proves to be unsuitable, it can easily be changed at this stage. A relatively low limit makes the program testing somewhat simpler.

The limitation that you have to enter a room number even when this is not used might appear an odd one. It is, however, based on experience of programming, as it allows one piece of code to read both entries. The program would be better if it did not ask for the room number when it is not used, and you might like to make these changes when you have read a few more chapters. In the design used here, however, the input takes place in a unit that, even with your limited knowledge so far, you are expected to understand and alter. The decisions, on the other hand, are made in code that is hidden from you at this stage. The section of code asking for the two inputs of menu choice and room number is therefore kept very simple to aid understanding.

Other decisions that have been made for the working program provided are that a welcome message will be displayed when the program is first run, and a farewell message will be displayed when the option to exit the program is chosen. The choices provided to the user are displayed in a menu. This offers option 1 to make a booking, after which a room number is entered. Option 2 on the menu allows an enquiry whether a room is available, with the room number again being requested after the entry of '2'. Option 3 will stop the running of the program. For the technical reasons explained above, a room number will also have to be entered before the choice is processed, but its value is ignored.

Various messages have been designed in the initial code provided. The choice of good messages for the user is another part of the specification that is not usually described in the user's requirements.

In this case, there are seven messages:

Message	Use of message
1　`Room n is now booked` (where n is a valid room number)	Displayed when a successful new booking is made
2　`Sorry, Room n is already booked` (where n is a valid room number)	Displayed when an attempt is made to book a room when that room has already been reserved
3　`Sorry that is not a valid room number to book`	Displayed when an attempt is made to book a room with a number that is outside the permitted range (1–20 according to the limitations stated above)
4　`Room n is booked` (where n is a valid room number)	Displayed when an enquiry is made about a specified room which is booked
5　`Room n is available` (where n is a valid room number)	Displayed when an enquiry is made about a specified room which is not booked
6　`Sorry that is not a valid room number to display`	Displayed when a request is made to display details of a room, but the room number given is out of range
7　`Sorry that is not a valid menu choice`	Displayed when a menu selection is made which is out of the required range

These seven messages are used as follows:

- The first three are used for choice 1 on the menu (add); the first follows a valid booking, the second explains that a new booking cannot be made because one already exists, and the third message explains that a new booking cannot be made because a valid room number has not been given.
- The next three are used for choice 2 on the menu (display); the first confirms that a booking exists for a valid room number given, the second confirms that a vacancy exists for a valid room number given, and the third message explains that a booking cannot be displayed because a valid room number has not been given.
- The seventh message is displayed when a choice other than 1, 2 or 3 is made.

4.2　Explanation of the files provided

There are four files used in this chapter. Three of them are new files, provided in the directory chap4:

hotel.pas

This is the main program. It calls procedures from the various units provided described below. It is provided as uncompiled source code and you must compile it before you can run it. You cannot do this, of course, until the various units that it uses have been successfully compiled.

hotutil.pas

This unit contains a number of procedures that have been written specially for this case study, and are unlikely to be useful for other case studies, as they are very specific to this case study. This file is provided in source code form, as you will be making changes to it.

hotbase.pas

This unit is provided as source code, but it is not intended that you read and understand it. After compiling utils.pas (see below), your first action during this case study will be to compile hotbase, hence producing hotbase.tpu, which you will subsequently use. The code contained within hotbase has been specially written for this case study. The statements used within it are beyond the scope of this chapter, which does not involve understanding or altering it. At a later stage, you would be able to understand the code.

utils.pas

The fourth file that you will need is utils.pas from the last case study, which should be copied into the chap4 directory as the first step in the exercises which follow. This, of course, assumes that you have produced a working version as part of your work in the previous chapter. If you have not done this, then you could use the utils.pas source code provided in the directory utils, but the procedures in it are in 'skeleton' form only. This means that whilst they will compile and execute, they are not in a finished or polished form. This 'fallback' file also contains code for procedures that you will be writing in later chapters, but as the current chapter does not use them, these can be ignored.

4.3 Getting the first version to work

The material that has been provided on disk has been prepared in such a way that you will be able to carry out the useful exercise of using existing Pascal code that will then be run and tested. Later in the chapter you will adapt and amend the code.

EXERCISE 4.1

Using the files provided, carry out the following steps, which should generate an executable program based on the code you were given. This will enable you to carry out the testing that you will be planning later.

Step 1. Copy utils.pas from your chap3 directory. Load Pascal and change directory to a:\chap4.

Step 2. Compile utils.pas. This will generate the file utils.tpu on your disk. (Note that you could have copied utils.tpu directly from a:\chap3.)

Step 3. Load and compile hotbase.pas. This will generate the file hotbase.tpu on your disk, provided that you remember to change the destination to disk.

Step 4. Compile hotutil.pas. This will generate the file hotutil.tpu on your disk, provided that you keep the destination as disk.

Step 5. Compile hotel.pas. This will generate hotel.exe on disk.

Step 6. Run the program hotel, following the dialogue and entering simple data to make a room booking, and then to check that the booking has been successful. At this stage, you are not attempting a formal test on the program, but are investigating the 'look and feel' of the program from the user's point of view.

Step 7. Run the program again, this time from Dos. (In order to do this you will need to exit from Turbo Pascal, and, if necessary, change the current directory to a:\chap4.)

The program as provided gives only a very basic dialogue. It will be part of your job later to improve on this. For now, however, you can start testing the program in its current form.

4.4   Testing the program – the planning stage

As mentioned in Chapter 3, programs must be tested thoroughly, and even for a simple problem such as this one, testing must be thoroughly planned. Unfortunately there are no short cuts to designing good test data. If a program is changed in any way, which it will be as you develop the code later in this case study, then the whole program must be re-tested.

The purpose of testing a program is to prove, as far as you can, that the program does what you claim it does. The emphasis, therefore, should be on demonstrating correctness, and should be mainly about testing that the program works when it is claimed that it works. Unfortunately, too many programmers find it easier to choose data that is complicated and might 'trick' the program into giving the wrong answer. Many test plans are devised which test all the peculiar and exceptional cases, but fail to test the ordinary working cases. The emphasis should be on ensuring that the program works when it should. At the end of a test plan, a few of the more complicated entries can be tried to see if the program is tripped up. As you probably won't find it difficult to think of these examples, relatively little will be said about this type of test data.

Test data for any problem can be classified in four types:

- data which is clearly valid
- data which is just valid
- data which is clearly invalid
- data which is just invalid.

This is the suggested order in which you design test data. It is no use in your first test trying data that is clearly not allowed. If the program fails to give the correct answer, this might be because it has detected the incorrect data, or it may fail to work whatever data it is given. So, the message is 'try valid data first'. As you work through a test plan, as you will see later, you may reach the point when the program you are testing goes wrong. This usually requires a correction to the program or units that it uses. The temptation is then to resume the test plan at the point where you left off, trying the last data set at which the previous test broke down. You should not do this. Whenever you make a change to a program, you should recommence the testing at the beginning of the test plan. The 'correction' you have made to solve one problem may cause other problems, so you should detect these early.

Ideally, testing of a program should include the entry of every possible input so that it can be verified that the program works in all cases. Even with a problem as apparently straightforward as the hotel booking, though, the entry of all possible inputs would be impractical. The art of testing, therefore, is to pick data that is typical of all possibilities. You might assume, for example, that if the system works properly to book rooms 15 and 17, then booking room 16 is very likely to work correctly. Strictly, room 16 should also be tested as it, alone, may go wrong.

Each time you test a program, you will use a set of test data. In the hotel booking example, you will need to make a booking before you can check whether a room is booked. What happens if checking a room accidentally deletes the booking? One way of checking this is to book a room, check that it is booked, and then check that it is booked again (and it should still be booked). Alternatively, you could book a room, check it is booked, and then try to book it again (which you should not be allowed to do unless it was accidentally cancelled). In this way, it is possible to test for several correct operations in one run of the program by one set of test data. Testing for error conditions, though, has to be carried out in separate tests, as you have to prove that each error on its own is enough to produce the correct reaction or error message.

Each set of test data has a purpose, though there may be several related purposes for one set of test data. For example, a set of test data might be used to show that checking a room booking does not alter a room booking, but at the same time it could be verifying that the highest room number can be used successfully. In writing a test plan, the purpose of each data set must be stated.

A set of test data must be precisely that. A test plan, showing each test to be carried out, should state the precise data, in order, which will be used. This will then enable somebody who has not read the program, and may not even have read the program specification, to run the test plan. In a large programming operation, the person who designs the test data would be completely separate from the person who writes the program. The test data designer would write the test plan from the program specification, not from reading the program.

The results of using a test plan should generate a table something like this:

Test number	Test data set	Purpose of test	Expected result	Actual result	Comment
1					
2					
3					
4					
5					

Tests should be numbered consecutively from 1. Each test data set should state precisely what should be typed. When the dialogue is complicated, you may need to include elements of the user dialogue between inputs to put your chosen inputs in context. Whatever you do, you should make it clear precisely what should be entered into the computer. The purpose of the test will describe the reasons for the test, perhaps describing the data as typical of a particular class of possible inputs.

The 'expected result' column should show precisely what the tester expects to happen with the given inputs. This should enable somebody using the plan to see precisely whether the expected result occurs.

These first four columns are usually described as the test plan. They are all written before the testing commences. The final two columns are used to record test results, so the six-column version of this table is known as the test log.

When a program is written to the specification, every entry in the 'actual result' column will say 'as expected'. Where the actual result is not as expected a test plan should state precisely what did occur. The comment column is then used to explain any difference between the expected result and the actual result.

There are several possibilities that could explain the difference between these two columns. The one that comes most readily to mind is that the programmer has not made the program do what it is supposed to do. There are other possible explanations as well, though. There may be forms of input that cause the program to crash because of the way errors are handled by Turbo Pascal. An obvious example which will emerge during this case study is the input of a fractional number, with a decimal point, when a whole number is expected. The 'comment' column could explain such a situation, and it would be up to the person commissioning the program to decide whether such a problem needs to be overcome. Another example of an entry in the comment column might describe a minor difference between the specified screen layout and the one that actually occurs with particular data. This could be commented on, particularly if a minor difference had not been foreseen when the program was specified.

Any test plan must bear in mind the original program requirements, the limitations that were then placed on this, and the messages that were chosen. Each aspect of these three categories should be included somewhere on the test plan.

4.5   Testing the program – the practical task

In later chapters, you will be required to write your own test plan, but in this case, a simple test plan is provided for you. In the next exercise, you will be applying this test plan, in one case to the working program that you have already used, in the other to a ready-compiled program provided on the disk that contains one or more errors.

In interpreting this test plan, it is worth bearing in mind that the program's menu looks like this:

> Do you want to:
> 1: Add a booking
> 2: Display bookings
> 3: Exit

The following table is a test plan, so the columns for 'Actual result' and 'Comment' are omitted though they would be included when the test results are generated.

Test number	Test data set		Purpose of test	Expected result
1	*(from menu, choose)*	1	To book a room, the	*At line 2, displays*
	(then type room)	1	lowest in the range,	`Room 1 is now booked`
	(from menu, choose)	2	check it is recorded as	*At line 4, displays*
	(then type room)	1	booked, then try to	`Room 1 is currently booked`
	(from menu, choose)	1	book the same room	*At line 6, displays*
	(then type room)	1	again (to provoke	`Sorry, Room 1 is already booked`
	(from menu, choose)	2	'booked' message),	*At line 8, displays*
	(then type room)	1	then to check it is still	`Room 1 is currently booked`
	(from menu, choose)	3	recorded as booked,	*At line 10, displays*
	(then type room)	1	then to exit	`Farewell`
				and program stops
2	*(from menu, choose)*	1	To book a room, the	*At line 2, displays*
	(then type room)	20	highest in the range,	`Room 20 is now booked`
	(from menu, choose)	2	check it is recorded as	*At line 4, displays*
	(then type room)	20	booked, then try to	`Room 20 is currently booked`
	(from menu, choose)	1	book the same room	*At line 6, displays*
	(then type room)	20	again (to provoke	`Sorry, Room 20 is already booked`
	(from menu, choose)	2	'booked' message),	*At line 8, displays*
	(then type room)	20	then to check it is still	`Room 20 is currently booked`
	(from menu, choose)	3	recorded as booked,	*At line 10, displays*
	(then type room)	20	then to exit	`Farewell`
				and program stops

Test number	Test data set		Purpose of test	Expected result
3	*(from menu, choose)*	1	To book two rooms,	*At line 2, displays*
	(then type room)	2	check the first is	Room 2 is now booked
	(from menu, choose)	1	recorded as booked (in	*At line 4, displays*
	(then type room)	5	case only the last	Room 5 is now booked
	(from menu, choose)	2	room booked is	*At line 6, displays*
	(then type room)	2	remembered), then try	Room 2 is currently booked
	(from menu, choose)	1	to book the same room	*At line 8, displays*
	(then type room)	2	again (to provoke	Sorry, Room 2 is already booked
	(from menu, choose)	2	'booked' message),	*At line 10, displays*
	(then type room)	5	then to check the other	Room 5 is currently booked
	(from menu, choose)	1	room is still recorded	*At line 12, displays*
	(then type room)	5	as booked, then try to	Sorry, Room 5 is already booked
	(from menu, choose)	3	book it again (to	*At line 14, displays*
	(then type room)	5	provoke 'booked'	Farewell
			message), then to exit	*and program stops*
4	*(from menu, choose)*	2	To check whether a	*At line 2, displays*
	(then type room)	3	room is marked as	Room 3 is currently available
	(from menu, choose)	1	booked before a	*At line 4, displays*
	(then type room)	3	booking request is	Room 3 is now booked
	(from menu, choose)	2	made, to make a	*At line 6, displays*
	(then type room)	3	booking for that room,	Room 3 is currently booked
	(from menu, choose)	3	and to check that it is	*At line 8, displays*
	(then type room)	3	then marked as	Farewell
			booked, then to exit	*and program stops*
5	*(from menu, choose)*	1	To book a room, and	*At line 2, displays*
	(then type room)	20	then check whether	Room 20 is now booked
	(from menu, choose)	2	various rooms are	*At line 4, displays*
	(then type room)	6	marked as booked,	Room 6 is currently available
	(from menu, choose)	2	including looking at	*At line 6, displays*
	(then type room)	6	one room more than	Room 6 is currently available
	(from menu, choose)	2	once, then to exit	*At line 8, displays*
	(then type room)	5		Room 5 is currently available
	(from menu, choose)	2		*At line 10, displays*
	(then type room)	9		Room 9 is currently available
	(from menu, choose)	3		*At line 12, displays*
	(then type room)	9		Farewell
				and program stops
6	*(from menu, choose)*	1	To make a room	*At line 2, displays*
	(then type room)	6	booking, to attempt to	Room 6 is now booked
	(from menu, choose)	1	book a room with a	*At line 4, displays*
	(then type room)	25	room number which is	Sorry that is not a valid room
	(from menu, choose)	2	too high, to check the	number to book
	(then type room)	6	original booking still	*At line 6, displays*
	(from menu, choose)	1	stands, to attempt to	Room 6 is currently booked
	(then type room)	0	book a room with a	*At line 8, displays*
	(from menu, choose)	2	room number which is	Sorry that is not a valid room
	(then type room)	6	too low, to check the	number to book

Test number	Test data set		Purpose of test	Expected result
6 cont.	(from menu, choose)	2	original booking still	*At line 10, displays*
	(then type room)	1	stands, to check a	`Room 6 is currently booked`
	(from menu, choose)	3	room which is not	*At line 12, displays*
	(then type room)	21	booked and to exit	`Room 1 is currently available`
			with a room number	*At line 14, displays*
			which is too large,	`Farewell`
			then to exit	*and program stops*
7	(from menu, choose)	1	To book a room, to	*At line 2, displays*
	(then type room)	7	select a menu option	`Room 7 is now booked`
	(from menu, choose)	0	which is too low (to	*At line 4, displays*
	(then type room)	0	provoke 'not a valid	`Sorry that is not a valid menu`
	(from menu, choose)	4	menu choice'	`choice`
	(then type room)	0	message), to select a	*At line 6, displays*
	(from menu, choose)	2	menu option which is	`Sorry that is not a valid menu`
	(then type room)	7	too high (to provoke	`choice`
	(from menu, choose)	1	'not a valid menu	*At line 8, displays*
	(then type room)	7	choice' message), to	`Room 7 is currently booked`
	(from menu, choose)	3	check existing	*At line 10, displays*
	(then type room)	2	booking still stands	`Sorry Room 7 is already booked`
			after false menu	*At line 12, displays*
			choices, to attempt to	`Farewell`
			book the same room	*and program stops*
			again, then to exit	
8	(from menu, choose)	1	To book a room, to	*At line 2, displays*
	(then type room)	8	select a menu option	`Room 8 is now booked`
	(from menu, choose)	0	which is too low (to	*At line 4, displays*
	(then type room)	6	provoke 'not a valid	`Sorry that is not a valid menu`
	(from menu, choose)	4	menu choice'	`choice`
	(then type room)	0	message), to select a	*At line 6, displays*
	(from menu, choose)	2	menu option which is	`Sorry that is not a valid menu`
	(then type room)	0	too high (to provoke	`choice`
	(from menu, choose)	2	'not a valid menu	*At line 8, displays*
	(then type room)	21	choice' message), to	`Sorry that is not a valid room`
	(from menu, choose)	2	attempt to display a	`number to display`
	(then type room)	8	booking for a room	*At line 10, displays*
	(from menu, choose)	3	number which is too	`Sorry that is not a valid room`
	(then type room)	2	low (to provoke 'not	`number to display`
			valid' display), to	*At line 12, displays*
			attempt to display a	`Room 8 is currently booked`
			booking for a room	*At line 14, displays*
			number which is too	`Farewell`
			high (to provoke 'not	*and program stops*
			valid' display), to	
			check existing	
			booking still stands	
			after false choices, then	
			to exit	

Test number	Test data set		Purpose of test	Expected result
9	*(from menu, choose)*	−2	To select a menu	*At line 2, displays*
	(then type room)	3	option which is too	`Sorry that is not a valid menu`
	(from menu, choose)	2	low (to provoke 'not a	`choice`
	(then type room)	3	valid menu choice'	*At line 4, displays*
	(from menu, choose)	1	message), to attempt	`Room 3 is currently available`
	(then type room)	3	to display a booking	*At line 6, displays*
	(from menu, choose)	2	for a room which has	`Room 3 is now booked`
	(then type room)	3	not been booked, to	*At line 8, displays*
	(from menu, choose)	9	book that room, to	`Room 3 is currently booked`
	(then type room)	21	display information	*At line 10, displays*
	(from menu, choose)	3.8	for that room, to	`Sorry that is not a valid menu`
	(then type room)	8	choose a menu option	`choice`
	(from menu, choose)	3	which is too high with	*At line 12, displays*
	(then type room)	2	a room number which	`Sorry that is not a valid menu`
			is too high, and to	`choice`
			attempt to choose	*At line 14, displays*
			from the menu with	`Farewell`
			an invalid type of	*and program stops*
			input (with a decimal	
			point), and to exit	

It is very clear that testing even a fairly simple program requires quite a complex test plan. In later case studies, you will be asked to write your own test plan. In this case, however, you are simply asked to use the one you are given.

When you use the test plan, test number 9 produces an error that you would not expect, as Turbo Pascal does not react to the decimal point in the way described in the test plan. The person carrying out the test plan would use the comment column in the test results to explain this.

EXERCISE 4.2

Step 1. Ensure that the units provided are all compiled and then the main program is compiled ready for running. (This should have been produced when you carried out Exercise 4.1.)

Step 2. Run the program 'hotel' with the test plan described above, noting the outcomes of each of the nine tests. If there are any departures from the expected results, then try to explain the reason.

Step 3. Run the program 'hotduff'. (This is provided as an EXE file.) This is a version that contains deliberate errors. By using the test plan, you should be able to spot these errors.

4.6 Examining the code provided – what does it teach us?

By reading the programs described in this book, you will be learning the rules of syntax of Turbo Pascal. This term is used to describe the rules of the language. In a similar way to that in which you learnt a natural language (such as English), the authors hope that by seeing Turbo Pascal used properly, you will get a feeling for its rules.

The main program that is written for you looks like this:

```
PROGRAM hotel;
{
    Main program for Chapter 4 - Hotel Booking
    Accepts room bookings and displays whether a room is booked
    Written by AMC/MPW
    1:1:96
}

USES hotutil, utils, hotbase;

VAR option, room : INTEGER;       {program variables to
                                   hold user's choices}

    bookings : HotelData;         {this data structure type
                                   is defined in 'hotbase'}

BEGIN
    RestoreColour;
    Welcome;
    {
      initialise variable 'option' which is used to control loop
    }
    option := 0;
    {
      initialise all rooms to vacant
    }
    InitialiseHotel(bookings);
    WHILE option <> 3 DO
    BEGIN
        DisplayMenu;
        AskFor(option, room);
        Process(option, room, bookings);
        Pause;
    END;   {WHILE}
    Farewell;
    RestoreColour
END.    {of hotel}
```

From the way that programs are presented, you will also encounter good practice in the layout of programs and techniques such as use of comments and indentation (leaving spaces at the start of lines). Programs will compile provided that you have used the rules of the language properly, irrespective of the program's presentation. The reason for good presentation, such as the use of comments and indentation, is for the benefit of the human reader. It is important for you to mimic the presentation of coding in this book to aid your programming in the future, particularly bearing in mind that other people will need to read your programs. When you have more programming experience, you might like to evolve your own conventions based on the ones used in this book.

Notice a number of aspects of this program:

The three units were described earlier. Many of the case studies used in this book use this same pattern of units.

One unit (hotbase) is provided as a complete library which you are asked to compile. This enables you to be provided with some very powerful routines that you can use, despite not being able to understand at this stage how they work. You are told what each of the routines will do, but not how they do it. At a later point, it would be instructive to see how this unit works, but at this stage it is sufficient to know what is in the unit so that it can be used.

A second unit (hotutil) contains specially written code for this case study, but it is simple enough that you are going to alter it to improve its appearance. These procedures are in 'skeleton' form, so they currently compile, but they should be replaced by better versions before the project is complete.

The third unit (utils) contains code written for Chapter 3, and now this is being used in a different context. The whole philosophy of this course is to recycle working code as much as possible when this is appropriate, so it makes sense from the start to store separately those routines that would be of wider use.

Each unit in Turbo Pascal consists of two parts, first the 'interface' section, then the 'implementation' section. The interface section contains all the information that is required to use the items in the unit. Where sections of code from hotbase are quoted below, they are from the interface section. The interface tells a user all that is necessary to use a procedure in the unit, for example. The convention to which all the code in this book is written suggests that a comment is included in the interface section of a unit for ease of understanding. Technically, from the compiler's point of view, it is only the declaration part, before the comment, which is strictly necessary.

In this case study, you are asked to alter hotutil. In the simple case given here, you are altering existing working procedures. This is done by amending the implementation section of a unit. In later case studies when, for example, you add a new procedure to a unit, you will need to add details of the procedure both to the interface and the implementation.

The convention also suggests that the full procedure heading in the interface is repeated in the implementation. This is not strictly necessary, but many would say that it improves readability. What must not occur, of course, is for the procedure heading in the two sections to be different. This will generate a compiler error.

Because all three units are used by the hotel program, all three must be compiled before they can be used by hotel.

The next part of the program consists of the variable declarations. The variables declared in a program allow data to be stored while the program is running. The main program variables are used to pass data to and receive data from the procedures that are used. In the structuring of any program, it is important to think about the scope of variables or other identifiers. The term 'scope' is used to describe the parts of the program for which it is meaningful to use the identifier. A variable declared in the main program can be used in the main program. Procedures in a unit cannot use a main program identifier as, when the unit is compiled, the main program may not be present, or indeed might not even be written. This aspect of Turbo Pascal, and the style in which it is used in this book, may appear frustrating at the moment, but is a key idea in producing well-written and structured code that can be re-used.

The data type 'integer' stores a single whole number. Each version of Pascal allows the storage of whole numbers within a specified range. The type integer is pervasive so need not be imported from any unit through a uses clause. The data type integer is also known as a simple type, because it cannot be broken down into any smaller elements. This contrasts with the structured types that will be introduced later, and pointer types which are a more advanced concept. In other words, the type is simple, because it cannot be made any simpler. The type HotelData is different, however. This is a type defined in the unit hotbase, and imported to those units that use it and into the main program as here. In order to use a variable of type HotelData, you do not need to know how the data is stored. When you look at how the procedures are declared in units, you will see that several of them use parameters of type HotelData.

After the declarations at the start of the program comes the first 'begin', and then the executable code.

The first action of the program is to call the procedure RestoreColour, which ensures that future output to the screen will be white.

The program then calls the procedure Welcome from utils. This can either be the version which you developed in Chapter 3, or you can use the version provided for you in skeleton form on the disk in the directory 'utils'. Notice that, like ClrScr, the Welcome procedure has no parameters.

The next two actions are the initialisation of the data. Most programs should start in this way. Variables are designed to contain data. If their contents are looked at by a program before it has placed any meaningful data in them, then the original, probably meaningless and unpredictable, values will be used. The value of 'option' is set to zero, using an assignment statement based around : =.

The assignment statement consists of a variable identifier, followed by : =, followed by an expression of the same type as the variable identifier. The notation : = is sometimes referred to as 'colon equals', but is usually read as 'becomes equal to'. A syntax error would be present if an expression rather than a variable identifier were on the left-hand side of the : =. The expression on the right-hand side might, however, be fairly complex. This will be evaluated by the compiled program before assigning the value to the variable named by the identifier.

In the second case a procedure InitialiseHotel is used, which will set all the entries of a variable type HotelData to the state where no bookings are held. A procedure is needed for this because HotelData is a user-defined type. This style of programming allows a programmer to use a variable of type HotelData, and to treat it like an object which can have various actions (or operations) carried out on it, like resetting all bookings. This can be done without access to the way in which the data structure HotelData is actually implemented.

It is essential for anybody who provides a data structure hidden in this way to provide a means of carrying out all the necessary operations on that data. In nearly all the examples that you will see, where a data structure is provided, so is a means of initialising it.

The description of InitialiseHotel is in the interface of hotbase.

```
PROCEDURE InitialiseHotel(VAR IHrooms : HotelData);
{
      Pre-condition:       none
      Action:              sets all rooms to vacant
      Post-condition:      parameter is returned with all elements
                           (rooms) in the data structure set to FALSE
                           (for vacant)
}
```

The pre-condition describes what condition must apply to data that is passed to the procedure. In this case, there is none – any information passed to the procedure is ignored.

The action describes what the procedure does. The name of a procedure should be chosen to reflect the action that takes place, so procedure names normally start with a verb.

The post-condition describes the condition that will apply to any data returned.

In the main program, after the initialisation of the data comes a construction known as a loop. A series of statements is sandwiched between a 'begin' and its matching 'end'. The begin comes immediately after the 'while ... do' clause. The series of statements between the begin and end may be carried out over and over again. As long as the condition in the while clause holds true, the series of statements will be carried out in the order given. Each time the set of statements has been completed, the condition in the while clause is tested to determine whether it is still true, in which case the statements are carried out again. If, on the other hand, the condition is not true, then the series of statements is not carried out, and execution continues at the statement after the 'end' that marks the end of the list of statements.

From this description, it will be clear that if the condition is not true initially, the list of statements will never be carried out. If, however, the condition remains true all the time, then the program will loop around these statements forever. It follows logically, therefore, that if the condition is initially true and a while loop is to terminate, the actions within the series of statements must affect the condition within the while clause in order to terminate the repetition.

The condition controlling this particular while loop contains the pair of symbols <>, which represent 'not equal to'. The loop in this particular program is therefore carried out while the value of the variable 'option' is not 3. In other words, any other value of 'option' will ensure its repetition. Once a value of 3 is entered, the loop is terminated.

Within the loop, four statements are executed.

First the menu is displayed. This procedure is defined in hotutil. It is currently a simple skeleton version that can later be replaced by a better one if necessary.

Its description is in the interface of hotutil.

```
PROCEDURE DisplayMenu;
{
      Pre-condition:       none
      Action:              displays the main menu listing choices of
                           action for user
      Post-condition:      none
}
```

Second, a procedure is called which asks the user for an option from the menu, and a room number. This is a call to the procedure defined in hotutil.

Its description in the interface of hotutil is as follows:

```
PROCEDURE AskFor(VAR AFchoice1, AFchoice2 : INTEGER);
{
      Pre-condition:       none - previously held values are overwritten
      Action:              asks user for and accepts menu selection and
                           then room number
      Post-condition:      returns menu selection as first parameter and
                           room number as second parameter
}
```

Notice that the values being passed to this procedure must be of integer type. The procedure can be called with any two integer variables. In the definition of AskFor in the 'interface' of hotutil, these are given the names AFchoice1 and AFchoice2. Any names could have been chosen, and in this case the convention used is that of prefixing the identifier with the initials of the procedure name. Wherever these values need to be referred to in the implementation, these two names, AFchoice1 and AFchoice2, are used. For this reason, they are called formal parameters. This reflects the situation that any name could be substituted throughout the procedure and its definition, and exactly the same action would take place.

For the third instruction within the loop, the procedure 'Process' is used, which has a description in the interface of hotbase as follows:

```
PROCEDURE Process(Pchoice1, Pchoice2 : INTEGER;
                  VAR Proombooked: HotelData);
{
      Pre-condition:      first parameter must contain menu choice
                          second parameter must contain room number
                          selected
                          third parameter must contain current booking
                          data
      Action:             if the menu choice is 1 or 2, and the room
                          chosen is valid, this procedure carries out
                          the operation chosen (book or display) and
                          displays confirmation that this has been done
                          or that it cannot be done.
                          If the room chosen is not valid, one of the
                          other messages is displayed.
                          If the menu choice is 3 (for exit),
                          no action is taken.
                          If the menu choice is not 1, 2 or 3, a
                          message to this effect is displayed
      Post-condition:     on return, third parameter contains current
                          booking data updated by new booking if
                          necessary
}
```

This description is, on the surface, somewhat more complicated. This procedure is at the core of the solution which is provided. Depending on the values which are passed to this procedure, one of the possible actions will take place. At this stage, it is not necessary for you to consider how it works, but you must get a clear idea of the description of what it does.

An alternative form of the Action given above would be to use a table format based on the seven possible messages described earlier.

The final procedure call within the 'while' loop is to Pause, which waits for a user to press the 'Enter' key and then clears the screen.

There are four procedure calls within the loop controlled by the while statement. These are then followed, after the end of the loop, by a call to procedure 'Farewell' in utils. Again, you may use your own version or copy the skeleton version from the directory 'utils'.

4.7   How the procedures in the units work

At this stage, no explanation will be given of how the unit hotbase works. It uses a number of advanced statements which have not yet been introduced to the reader. One very important point about hotbase, however, is emphasised by the compilation of its ready-written source code. Indeed, hotbase might have been supplied purely as a tpu file which could then have been used, but not altered. A programmer who wished to use such a unit would need to be given details of the interface, but need not be told about the implementation.

In other words, a library can be used without understanding *how* it works, but merely from a description of *what* it does. This idea lies at the core of the approach to top-down programming, but still comes as a surprise to many people learning programming. Yet this also happens when you use statements like ReadLn and WriteLn, as these have the same form as procedures in a library. By carefully reading about what they do, and how to use them, most programmers are happy to apply them in a program without worrying about how they work. The same should apply to ready-written units like hotbase though, of course, you will test thoroughly any program which uses a ready-written procedure.

The unit hotutil is described so that it can be adapted in the exercises which follow.

The code for 'DisplayMenu', in the implementation section of hotutil, reads as follows.

```
PROCEDURE DisplayMenu;

BEGIN
    WriteLn('Do you want to:');
    WriteLn('1: Add a booking');
    WriteLn('2: Display bookings');
    WriteLn('3: Exit')
END;    {DisplayMenu}
```

The same procedure is used four times here. 'WriteLn' is a pervasive procedure which, like a procedure imported from a unit, can be used repeatedly. Unlike a procedure in a unit, however, it does not have to be specially requested in a uses clause; there is no unit in which it is declared.

The implementation part of procedure AskFor in hotutil, looks like this:

```
PROCEDURE AskFor(VAR AFchoice1, AFchoice2 : INTEGER);

BEGIN
    ReadLn(AFchoice1);
    WriteLn('Which room (1-20)');
    ReadLn(AFchoice2)
END;    {AskFor}
```

This again uses the WriteLn statement. The other statement used here is ReadLn. This allows for the input of data into the variable whose identifier is shown in brackets.

EXERCISE 4.3

In the previous exercises, you have compiled the versions of hotutil and utils with which you were supplied, then compiled and run hotel. In this further set of exercises, you will be asked both to make changes to some of these files, and to make some deliberate mistakes, in order to see their effect. This is important so that when, as will inevitably happen, you make mistakes which you did not intend, you will be familiar with the error messages which the system provides.

Before starting this exercise, copy your working versions of hotutil, utils and hotel into a separate directory with a title like safe, so that, however wrong things go, you know you have a safe backup to look at.

Step 1. Try loading hotutil, compiling it, then running it. You should get a message explaining that you cannot run a unit. This is because a unit contains only definitions which are then used elsewhere. Only a program can be run. You may make the mistake of trying to run a unit from time to time, because you get into the habit, when using programs, of compiling then running them. You will kick yourself when you do it, but attempting to run a unit does no harm.

Step 2. Make new copies of the various units in source code only (that is just the pas files). Try compiling them in a different order from that specified in Exercise 4.1. Make notes of the errors which occur, particularly when you attempt to compile code which uses another unit. Observe what happens if the unit being used has not been compiled.

Step 3. Make changes to 'DisplayMenu' in hotutil to improve the user dialogue. Repeat the process above so that hotel can again be run with the changes incorporated.

4.8   Describing the relationships between units

You have already seen that the order of compilation of the various units which you are using is very important. The unit hotbase was compiled first. This was a ready-written unit which you did not alter, and on which other units depend. The unit crt is potentially used by several other units. Because it is a system unit it need never be recompiled.

It is important to get a clear picture of the relationship between the different units. If their relationship is not designed carefully, there could be two units, each of which uses the other, and therefore both would have to be compiled first! This is clearly impossible.

One way of describing the relationship between units is to use a unit dependency diagram, as illustrated here for the current case study:

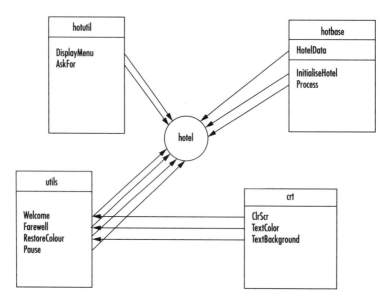

You will notice that each separate unit is identified in a separate box. There are three types of unit, but they are all represented in the same way.

- crt is a system unit, supplied with Turbo Pascal in a pre-compiled form;

- hotbase is a unit specially written by the authors of this case study, supplied to you as Pascal source code;
- utils and hotutil are specially written for this case study, but as part of it, you have altered the source code to improve the final program.

The arrows from the units to the program hotel show which items from the units are imported. Within units are shown, below the title, first any data structures (in this case HotelData), and then procedures.

The only data structure in the diagram is shown as being imported to the program so that the program can store data of this form. (In later case studies, explanations are given of how such data is stored. At this stage, it is important to see that a data structure can be used without understanding how it is implemented.)

Notice also that as the procedures TextColor, ClrScr and TextBackground are used in the unit utils (if you have implemented them), they are shown as being passed across. Because crt is a library which is ready-written, it will obviously not have any arrows pointing to it, as it cannot depend on units written by the programmer. In this particular situation, no procedures in crt are used directly in the program, but in principle, there is no problem with that. This particular case study could be said to use procedures in crt indirectly.

Note that hotel is not a unit, it is a program, and it is therefore shown as a different shape (a circle). You have not altered the program during this case study, but there is nothing to stop you doing this to enhance the program. The unit dependency diagram is intended to show on which units the program depends and which units depend on which other units. This has two purposes. First, it ensures that the correct uses clauses are present in the units – any units from which a program or unit imports are clearly seen as those from which arrows arrive. Secondly, the relationship of units is clear so that the order of compilation is easy to determine – if arrows come into a unit from another unit, then that other unit must be compiled first. In the case of system units, they do not need to be recompiled because they are not altered.

The idea of unit dependency diagrams is used in later chapters to ensure solutions are properly designed.

4.9 Adding some colour

Further changes can be made to the existing procedures by introducing text in colour. In order to do this, you should use the procedure TextColor as described in Chapter 3.

The various identifiers for colours Red, Blue and so on are defined in the unit crt, and their values are imported from there when used. (See also Appendix 1.)

EXERCISE 4.4

Step 1. Adapt DisplayMenu so that the menu is displayed in green, but all other text is in white. Remember that any altered unit has to be recompiled, as does a program or unit which uses it.
(Hint: this involves TextColor statements at the top and bottom of DisplayMenu, or the use of RestoreColour from utils.)

Step 2. Adapt your personalised welcome message so that it appears in a colour of your choice. Run the program to check that your changes work.

Step 3. Adapt your personalised farewell message so that it appears in a colour of your choice different from the colour of your welcome message. Run the program to check that your changes work.

Step 4. Draw a new unit dependency diagram so that the changes you have just made, such as the additional procedures which you have used, are reflected in the diagram.

EXERCISE 4.5

These exercises are designed to help you to test yourself on the knowledge which you should have acquired in reading this chapter and doing the previous exercises.

1. Explain what is meant by a variable.
2. Describe in your own words the purpose of pre-condition, action and post-condition comments.
3. Explain why the order of compilation of units is important.
4. Explain why the convention of indenting lines of code is used in code written for this book.
5. Explain the use of the : = in a program and explain what can appear on the left-hand side of this symbol.
6. Why has the procedure DisplayMenu no parameters?
7. Explain what is meant by the term 'formal parameters'.
8. Describe four types of test data.
9. Explain the purpose of test plans.
10. Describe how a program can carry out the same series of statements several times, and how this repetition is terminated.

5

Personal identification numbers

Before starting this chapter, you should be able to do the following:

- use the Turbo Pascal environment to edit, and compile programs and units, and run programs
- write and use test plans
- use unit dependency diagrams
- use pre-written procedures from their interface descriptions.

Before tackling this chapter you should have produced a utilities unit containing:

- Welcome
- Farewell
- Pause
- RestoreColour.

After tackling this chapter you should understand:

- the use of Pascal selection (if) statements
- the use of the arithmetic operators 'mod' and 'div' and the logical operators 'and' and 'or'
- the difference between formal and actual parameters
- the difference between value and var parameters
- how to write procedures.

After tackling this chapter you will have produced a utilities unit containing:

- Welcome
- Farewell
- Pause
- RestoreColour
- AskForPin
- CheckPin.

5.1 Introduction to PINs

Personal identification numbers (PINs) are becoming increasingly common. You may need one to draw money from a cash machine, to activate a photocopying card, or to gain access to a computer room in College. Computers are often used to validate these numbers, and this case study considers a program to perform this validation task.

5.2   Understanding the problem

A program is required that determines whether an identification number that a potential user of a computer types in is valid, and prints an appropriate message.

EXERCISE 5.1

Step 1. Have you been given sufficient information to solve the problem?

Step 2. Make a list of anything else you might need to know.

Clearly, you as the programmer need to know the rule which determines whether a number is valid or not. You also need to know whether there are to be any limits on the range of numbers allowed.

It has been decided that valid identification numbers will be positive integers containing four digits and no leading zeros. That means that, for example, 9000 would be a possible choice but 0009 would not. Further, identification numbers will only be valid if the following is true:

the sum of the first three digits modulo 9 equals the fourth digit.

(Note – modulo means the remainder after integer division is performed.)
Thus, the numbers 1350 and 8864 would be valid, because:

$1 + 3 + 5 = 9$ and $9 \div 9 = 1$ remainder 0 so the remainder equals the fourth digit;
$8 + 8 + 6 = 22$ and $22 \div 9 = 2$ remainder 4 so the remainder again equals the fourth digit;

whereas 1461 and 6389 would be invalid, because:

$1 + 4 + 6 = 11$ and $11 \div 9 = 1$ remainder 2 so the remainder does not equal the fourth digit;
$6 + 3 + 8 = 17$ and $17 \div 9 = 1$ remainder 8 so again the remainder does not equal the fourth digit.

EXERCISE 5.2

Step 1. Are these identification numbers valid?
   4150   2362   9555   1359   9876

Step 2. Suppose the check digit were determined by dividing by 7 rather than 9. Find a four-digit code whose check digit would be correct in either system.

Step 3. The International Standard Book Number, or ISBN uses a check digit. Find out how the check digit is calculated, and try the method using the ISBN of two or three books. What other information is stored in the ISBN?

5.3   A possible solution

A program has been written, which will prompt the user for an identification number and then print a message granting or denying access to the computer according to whether or not the input code was valid.

EXERCISE 5.3

Step 1. Run the program which you will find as chap5\verify1.exe on your tutorial disk, from Dos or Windows.

Step 2. Test it, to make sure it works. Remember to devise a test plan first. Record the data you use, and your prediction of what should happen, as well as the actual output.
   Test the program with valid codes such as 1214, invalid codes such as 5219, and also illegal codes such as 12341 and 0092.

Step 3. Make a note of any alterations which may need to be made to the program.

5.4   Inspecting the solution

Once you are sure that you know what the problem is, you can start to write the algorithm for solving it. An algorithm is a set of instructions; it gives a series of steps to follow.
   There are three main steps for this problem:

Input: get the identification number from the user by
           (a) prompting for input
           (b) reading the input.

Process: determine if the identification number is valid.

Output: print an appropriate message.

Here is the Pascal code for verify1:

```
PROGRAM verify1;
{
   Main program for Chapter 5
   Validates a 4 digit identification number entered from the
   keyboard, and prints an appropriate message
   Written by AMC/MPW
   1:1:96
}

USES veribase, utils;

VAR  idnumber : INTEGER;
     isvalid  : BOOLEAN;

BEGIN
   Welcome;
   AskFor(idnumber);
   Check(idnumber, isvalid);
   DisplayMessage(isvalid);
   Pause;
   Farewell;
   RestoreColour
END.    {verify1}
```

EXERCISE 5.4

Step 1. Load Pascal, and change to the directory chap5.

Step 2. Type in the program above, compile and run it. Remember to record your test data, predicted and actual results.

Step 3. Save the program as verify1.pas.

Step 4. Experiment by introducing errors, one at a time, into your program. Record your findings.

5.5   Investigating units

Here is the Pascal code for the unit veribase:

```
UNIT veribase;
{
    procedures for use with verify.pas, for requesting a code,
    checking its validity, and displaying a message
    AMC/MPW
    1:1:96
}

INTERFACE

PROCEDURE AskFor(VAR AFnum : INTEGER);
{
    pre-condition:        none
    action:               requests and accepts an integer AFnum from
                          the keyboard
    post-condition:       AFnum contains the integer requested
}
PROCEDURE Check(Cnum : INTEGER; VAR Cok : BOOLEAN);
{
    pre-condition:        Cnum is a 4 digit integer
    action:               determines whether Cnum is valid and stores
                          the result in Cok.
                          Cnum is valid if its fourth digit equals the
                          sum of its first 3 digits modulo 9
    post-condition:       Cok is TRUE if Cnum is valid, FALSE otherwise
}
PROCEDURE DisplayMessage(DMok : BOOLEAN);
{
    pre-condition:        DMok is a Boolean
    action:               displays message about the validity of an id
                          number depending on value of DMok
    post-condition:       none

}
```

```
IMPLEMENTATION

PROCEDURE AskFor(VAR AFnum : INTEGER);

BEGIN
   Write('Please type in a four-digit identification number:');
   ReadLn(AFnum)
END; {AskFor}

PROCEDURE Check(Cnum : INTEGER; VAR Cok : BOOLEAN);

VAR  lCdigit1, lCdigit2, lCdigit3, lCcheckdigit,
     lCremainder : INTEGER;

BEGIN
   lCcheckdigit := Cnum MOD 10;
   lCdigit1 := Cnum DIV 1000;
   lCdigit2 := (Cnum DIV 100) MOD 10;
   lCdigit3 := (Cnum DIV 10) MOD 10;
   lCremainder := (lCdigit1 + lCdigit2 + lCdigit3) MOD 9;
   IF lCremainder = lCcheckdigit THEN
   BEGIN
      Cok := TRUE
   END
   ELSE
   BEGIN
      Cok := FALSE
   END
END; {Check}

PROCEDURE DisplayMessage(DMok : BOOLEAN);

BEGIN
   IF DMok THEN
   BEGIN
      WriteLn('The number is valid. Access granted.')
   END
   ELSE
   BEGIN
      WriteLn('*** The number is not valid. Access denied.')
   END
END; {DisplayMessage}

END.    {veribase}
```

A unit begins with the unit header, the word 'unit' followed by an identifier. The file which contains the unit must have the same name as the unit, so that the compiler can find it when compiling a program which uses it. Thus, the unit veribase will be stored in the Pascal file veribase.pas. When the unit is compiled, the compiler creates a file with the extension .tpu (for Turbo Pascal unit). It is this compiled version of the unit which is used by other libraries or programs.

Notice also that the unit terminates with the word 'end', followed by a full stop. This 'end' has no corresponding 'begin', as the unit consists entirely of procedure declarations and has no action part.

5.6   The interface section

The unit is in two parts: the interface and the implementation sections. The interface must contain a list of any constants, types, procedures and functions which may be accessed by other units and programs. In this case study, there will only be procedures in the unit. It should also contain an explanation of what each procedure and function does, so that someone can use the unit just by reading the interface, without having to wade through the code in the implementation section as well. This book uses the convention of pre-condition, action, and post-condition to describe a procedure. The 'pre-condition' is the information which must be available to the procedure when it is activated, and the 'post-condition' is the new information which the procedure makes available as it terminates. The 'action' is a description of what the procedure actually does.

For example, in the unit veribase there are three procedures listed in the interface section:

AskFor, Check, and DisplayMessage.

AskFor has no pre-condition, as the procedure does not need any information when it is first activated. The action of the procedure is that a message is output requesting a code, which is input from the keyboard. This code must be made available to the calling program (i.e. verify1). Thus, the integer is returned by way of the var parameter, and the post-condition states that AFnum will contain the requested integer.

Check has both pre- and post-conditions. The four-digit code needs to be known when the procedure is activated, so that is a pre-condition. The code will not be altered by the procedure, so a value parameter is used to pass the code. The action of the procedure is to determine whether the code is valid, and the result, a Boolean (set to True or False), needs to be available to the calling program. The Boolean is returned by a var parameter, and the post-condition states that Cok will contain this result.

DisplayMessage has only a pre-condition. The message to be displayed needs to be known when the procedure is activated, but is not going to be altered by the procedure. It is therefore passed as a value parameter. The action is to display the message on the screen. No new information is available at the end of the procedure, so there is no post-condition.

EXERCISE 5.5

Draw the unit dependency diagram for this program.

5.7   Parameters

The pre- and post-conditions are closely related to the parameters, which hold data to be accessed and manipulated in the procedure. Information should be communicated between calling program and procedure only via the parameter list, so that procedures are entirely self-contained. This is an important feature of modular programming. Look at the procedure headings again:

```
PROCEDURE AskFor(VAR AFnum: INTEGER);

PROCEDURE Check(Cnum: INTEGER; VAR Cok: BOOLEAN);

PROCEDURE DisplayMessage(DMok: BOOLEAN);
```

Pascal distinguishes two kinds of parameter – value and var parameters. A value parameter is one which contains information needed when the procedure is activated; a var parameter contains new information available at the end of execution of the procedure.

Consider the four-digit code 'idnumber' used in verify1. It is new information obtained in AskFor, so must be a var parameter; however, this same information is needed from outside when Check is executed, so it must be a value parameter there. Similarly the Boolean 'isvalid' is new information obtained in Check, so must be a var parameter, but it is information needed from outside when DisplayMessage is executed, and so it must be a value parameter there. Pascal uses the reserved word 'var' to denote var parameters in procedure declarations, as can be seen in the three declarations above.

```
PROCEDURE AskFor(VAR AFnum: INTEGER);
```

has one parameter, an integer, which is a var parameter.

```
PROCEDURE Check(Cnum: INTEGER; VAR Cok: BOOLEAN);
```

has two parameters, a value parameter which is an integer, and a var parameter which is a Boolean.

```
PROCEDURE DisplayMessage(DMok : BOOLEAN);
```

has one parameter, a Boolean, which is a value parameter.

The parameters used when declaring a procedure are called formal parameters. Identifiers are chosen which represent the actual parameters that will be used when the procedure is activated by a program (or even by another procedure). The convention is used in this book that the names of formal parameters should start with the initial letters of the procedure name. Figure 5.1 shows how the formal parameters used within the procedures declared in veribase relate to the actual parameters used in verify1.

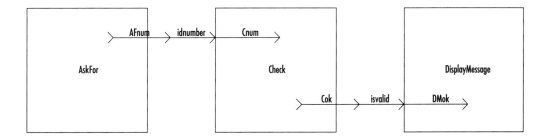

Figure 5.1

Each procedure is self-contained, and so the formal parameters of one procedure have no direct communication at all with the formal parameters of any other procedure; the actual parameters used when the procedures are called contain the data in the main program. Thus, the declaration of AskFor is:

```
PROCEDURE AskFor(VAR AFnum: INTEGER);
```

where AFnum is the formal parameter.

When AskFor is called, or activated, in the program, the actual parameter idnumber is used:

```
AskFor(idnumber);
```

and after the procedure has been executed, idnumber (the actual parameter, declared as a variable in the main program) contains the value of the four-digit code.

The validity of the code can then be checked by calling Check with idnumber (which contains the code) as the actual parameter for that procedure.

Different programs, or different procedures used by one program, may need to call the same procedure. Any actual parameter can be used, provided it is of the correct type to match the formal parameter.

Sometimes data is changed by a procedure. The value of the data is needed when the procedure is activated, but at the end of execution of the procedure new data is available. Pascal does not have a third type of parameter for this case, but uses var parameters for both new and changed information at the end of a procedure. An example of this occurred in Chapter 4, the hotel case study. When a request is made to book a room, the booking procedure needs to know whether the room has already been booked, so that information must be available when the procedure is called. But by the end of execution of the procedure, the 'booked status' of a room may have changed, and so this information needs to be made available to the calling program. Thus, a var parameter must be used for this data.

5.8 The implementation section

The interface section describes how to use the procedures in the unit, together with comments explaining what the procedures do. The implementation section contains the code, telling the computer how to do whatever is required. A procedure declaration looks very similar to a program, with the same structure of header, declaration part and action part.

If variables are needed by the procedure, for local use only inside the procedure, then they should be declared at the start of the procedure in the same way as program variables are declared at the start of a program. The convention is used in this book that all such local variables start with lower case 'l' (for local) followed by the initial letters of the procedure name. So in the procedure Check, the local variables are given names beginning 'lC', such as 'lCdigit1' and 'lCremainder'. The only variables which should appear in a procedure will be either local variables or formal parameters.

A procedure can, of course, call another procedure. The action part of AskFor contains two procedure calls, to the pervasive procedures Write and ReadLn which you have already met. The syntax of the other two procedures is discussed in the following sections.

Finally, a unit can be regarded as a set of recipes. It tells the computer what code to execute should a program require a particular procedure.

5.9 Integer arithmetic

Pascal distinguishes between two different number types. The 'integer' type refers to whole numbers, and has been encountered in previous chapters. The other number type is called 'real', and refers to numbers which contain a decimal point. Real numbers will feature in the statistics case study of Chapter 6. Computers store numbers as their binary representations, and so the two number types are stored quite differently. Integers can be represented exactly, but real numbers can only be represented approximately, as there is no exact binary equivalent to decimal numbers such as 0.1.

As you would expect, Pascal provides the standard arithmetic operations of addition, subtraction, multiplication and division. Addition, subtraction and multiplication are quite straightforward, producing answers which may be integer if both the operands are integer, and real otherwise. Integer values can be assigned to real variables, where they will be converted, but real values cannot be directly assigned to integers. Mixed arithmetic, involving both integer and real operands, is allowed, with the answer always being a real number. For example, the result of adding the integer 2 to the real number 1.5 would be the real number 3.5.

Given the declarations:

```
VAR   int1,  int2, int3, int4 :   INTEGER;
      re1,   re2,  re3,  re4  :   REAL;
```

the following assignments would be allowed:

```
int1 := 6;  int2 := 5;    int3 := 4 * int1;       int4 := int1 + int2;
re1  := 2;  re2  := 3.5;  re3  := 5*(re1 + 8.2);  re4  := int4 −re3;
```

where the * is used as the multiplication symbol.

But the following assignments would be illegal:

```
int1 := 2.5;   int2 := re1;   int3 := re4 − int4;
```

Division is a more complicated operation, in that we can choose to have a real or an integer answer. For example,

$7 \div 2$ has the alternative answers 3.5 or 3 remainder 1.

Pascal distinguishes between these two possibilities by offering two distinct types of division.

Real division uses the operator '/' and the answer is always a real. The operands may be real or integer or a mixture. Thus

```
7 / 2,   7.0 / 2,   7 / 2.0   and   7.0 / 2.0   all give the result 3.5.
```

Integer division requires both operands to be integer, and the two operators DIV and MOD are used to give, respectively, the whole number part and the remainder of the division. So

```
7 DIV 2   gives 3,   and   7 MOD 2   gives 1.
```

Given the Pascal variable declarations above, the following assignments would be allowed, as the results are all of type integer:

```
int1 := int2 MOD int3;    int4 := int2 DIV int3;
int2 := 47 DIV int1;      int3 := int3 MOD 10;
```

These assignments would also be allowed, as the results are all real:

```
re1 := re2 / re3;   re4 := re2 / 6.3;   re3 := 56 / re2;   re2 := 191 / 25;
```

However, the following assignments would not be allowed, as an integer variable cannot store a number of type real:

```
int1 := int2 / int4;   int3 := re1 / re2;   int2 := int3 / 2;
```

EXERCISE 5.6

Step 1. What is the result of the following operations?

(a)   27 DIV 4
(b)   27 MOD 4
(c)   15 MOD 3
(d)   15 MOD 7
(e)   11 DIV 11

Step 2. Given the variable declarations

VAR num1, num2, num3 : INTEGER;

and the assignments

num1 := 23;   num2 := 6;   num3 := 12;

what is the result of the following operations?

(a)   num1 DIV num2
(b)   num3 DIV num2
(c)   num1 MOD num3
(d)   17 MOD num2
(e)   num3 MOD 9

Step 3. In procedure Check, the first five lines of 'action' are:

```
lCcheckdigit := Cnum MOD 10;
lCdigit1 := Cnum DIV 1000;
lCdigit2 := (Cnum DIV 100) MOD 10;
lCdigit3 := (Cnum DIV 10) MOD 10;
lCremainder := (lCdigit1 + lCdigit2 + lCdigit3) MOD 9;
```

Choose three four-digit numbers, and work through the sequence of statements above for each of them.

5.10   Making a selection

In the second half of procedure Check, and in procedure DisplayMessage, a choice has to be made between two alternatives. The Pascal syntax for this is:

```
IF <condition> THEN
BEGIN
   <statements to execute if condition is true>
END
ELSE
BEGIN
   <statements to execute if condition is false>
END
```

Notice that no semicolons are needed within this structure. However, semicolons would be needed to separate the 'statements to execute' if there were more than one of them.

Sometimes there will be no need for the 'else' part of this structure, in which case it may be omitted, just as it is in English when the alternative of 'else do nothing' is not actually stated. For example, the advice 'If it looks like rain, then take an umbrella' does not need the additional advice 'otherwise don't take an umbrella'.

EXERCISE 5.7

The system administrator has decided to change the computer access codes. Valid codes must also have the first three digits all different from each other.

Write an algorithm for testing this. Do not worry about Pascal syntax for this, just try to write out a suitable test in English.

5.11 Multiple conditions – nested ifs

There are two ways of tackling Exercise 5.7 in Pascal. Firstly, the 'if' statement allows a choice between two possibilities, but further choices may be made by nesting additional if statements inside the first one.

```
IF digit1 <> digit2 THEN
BEGIN
    IF digit1 <> digit3 THEN
    BEGIN
        IF digit2 <> digit3 THEN
        BEGIN
            {they are all different so we can set a Boolean to TRUE}
            aredifferent := TRUE
        END
        ELSE
        BEGIN
            aredifferent := FALSE
        END
    END
    ELSE
    BEGIN
        aredifferent := FALSE
    END
END
ELSE
BEGIN
    aredifferent := FALSE
END
```

It would be very easy to miss a 'begin' or 'end' from this long and complicated-looking structure, but careful use of indentation ensures that every begin lines up with its corresponding end, and so a missing end should be fairly easy to spot. You will notice that 'aredifferent' is set to 'true' if all three digits turn out to be different, but has to be set to 'false' in the three other cases. It is possible to save some coding by setting aredifferent to 'false' at the beginning, and only changing it to 'true' if necessary. This simplifies the code, as all the 'else' clauses are no longer needed:

```
aredifferent := FALSE;
IF digit1 <> digit2 THEN
BEGIN
   IF digit1 <> digit3 THEN
   BEGIN
      IF digit2 <> digit3 THEN
      BEGIN
         {they are all different so we can set a Boolean to TRUE}
         aredifferent := TRUE
      END
   END
END
```

Simpler code is always easier to read, and much less prone to errors. If one of two conditions is more likely to occur, it often simplifies the code to assume at the beginning that this will be the case, and set the variable to that value. Then perform the test, and only reset the variable if necessary. This is a useful technique in a number of situations.

5.12   Logical and relational operators

An alternative to using a set of nested if statements is to use one of the logical operators which are provided by Pascal. Pascal provides three logical operators: 'not', 'and', and 'or' which can be used to combine expressions in a Boolean expression such as the condition required here. Again, there is a choice of several ways of implementing the test that all three digits are different.

Using 'and' operators, you can test that digit1 is not the same as digit2, and that digit2 is not the same as digit3, and that digit3 is not the same as digit1. If all these conditions hold, then aredifferent is 'true'. The Pascal code for this test is:

```
IF (digit1 <> digit2) AND (digit1 <> digit3)
   AND (digit2 <> digit3) THEN
BEGIN
   aredifferent := TRUE
END
ELSE
BEGIN
   aredifferent := FALSE
END
```

Using 'or' operators, you can test whether digit1 is the same as digit2, or digit 2 is the same as digit3, or digit3 is the same as digit1. If any of these conditions hold, then aredifferent is 'false'. The Pascal code for this is:

```
IF (digit1 = digit2) OR (digit1 = digit3)
   OR (digit2 = digit3) THEN
BEGIN
   aredifferent := FALSE
```

```
END
ELSE
BEGIN
    aredifferent := TRUE
END
```

Notice firstly that it is only possible to combine two operands together in the test for equality or inequality. You cannot, for example, test (digit1 = digit2 = digit3) in one operation.

Secondly, the operands need to be placed in parentheses, or round brackets. This is because of the precedence rules for logical operators. Precedence rules are used to decide the order in which operators are applied in a complex expression. You are probably already familiar with the precedence rules for arithmetic operators, commonly known as 'BODMAS'. In an arithmetic expression, the operations are carried out in order

1. <u>B</u>rackets
2. <u>O</u>f
   <u>D</u>ivision
   <u>M</u>ultiply
3. <u>A</u>dd
   <u>S</u>ubtract

so that, for example 3 + 4 * 2 gives the answer 11, because the precedence rules require the multiplication to be done first, 4 * 2 = 8 and then the addition, 3 + 8 = 11; while (3 + 4) * 2 gives the answer 14, because the precedence rules require the bracket to be evaluated first, (3 + 4) = 7, followed by the multiplication 7 * 2 = 14.

Similarly, precedence rules apply to logical operators, but there is no generally agreed precedence order, and so the rules vary between different programming languages. For Pascal the rule is:

highest precedence:	NOT
	AND * / DIV MOD
	OR + −
lowest precedence:	= <> < <= >=

where the lowest precedence operators (=, <>, etc.) are known as the relational operators.

Operations at the same level are performed left to right.

So if brackets are not used in expressions such as

```
digit1 = digit2 OR digit3 = digit4
```

the precedence rules mean that the first operation attempted will be

```
digit2 OR digit3
```

which in this context is meaningless. Parentheses, or round brackets, are required:

```
(digit1 = digit2) OR (digit3 = digit4)
```

to ensure that (digit1 = digit2) is evaluated first. The answer to this will be a Boolean value, 'true' or 'false'. Then (digit3 = digit4) will be evaluated, again resulting in a Boolean value. Finally the 'or' operator can be applied to the two Boolean values. If one or the other, or both, of them is 'true' then the whole expression is 'true'.

EXERCISE 5.8

Step 1. Write a procedure for checking that the first three digits of a four-digit code are all different, using one of the methods discussed above. Call this new procedure CheckDifferent. Use the procedure Check as a pattern, as the parameters and some of the code will be very similar.

Step 2. Add your new procedure to the interface and implementation sections of the unit veribase.pas. Remember to add pre-condition, action and post-condition comments, so that another user can use the procedure without having to read the implementation code for it.

Step 3. Use a different algorithm for checking whether the digits are different. Write a procedure for this check, give it a suitable name, and add it to the unit.

Step 4. Modify the main program verify1, so that if a code passes Check it is further tested in CheckDifferent. Save the new program as verify2.pas. Check that it compiles and runs.

Step 5. Modify the main program again, so that it uses the other procedure, produced in Step 3. The two procedures are interchangeable; they do the same job, and have the same interface. There is often more than one way of coding a procedure to perform a particular task. Another user of the procedure only needs to know about the interface, and does not need the details of exactly which method was used to code it.

Step 6. Prepare a test plan, and test the new program thoroughly, recording your findings.

There are many possible variations on the theme of valid codes and check digits. Another test states that a code is valid if the fourth digit is equal to the sum of the first three digits divided by 5. This time, the 'div' operator is required for the algorithm.

Using this algorithm, 1351 would be a valid code because

1 + 3 + 5 = 9 and
9 DIV 5 = 1

but 4567 would not be a valid code, because

4 + 5 + 6 = 15 and
15 DIV 5 = 3.

EXERCISE 5.9

Step 1. Write a procedure to test identification numbers which are valid if the fourth digit is equal to the sum of the first three digits divided by 5, and add it to veribase.pas.

Step 2. Write a program to use the new procedure. You will be able to recycle most of the existing code of verify1.pas. Save the new program as verify3.pas.

Step 3. Compile, run and test your program.

5.13   Character codes

After complaints from users, it has been decided to issue four-letter passwords rather than numeric codes. The program needs modifying again!

A variable of the Pascal type 'char' can be used to hold a single letter, so instead of reading one four-digit integer, the program must read four chars.

Valid codes will have all four letters the same, e.g. AAAA or zzzz. But just to complicate matters further, the boss has decided to have his own identification sequence – BOSS. When this code is entered, he wants a special message displayed; he is leaving it to you to choose appropriate wording.

EXERCISE 5.10

Look at the algorithms you have used already in this case study. How will they need to be changed? You will need to think carefully about how you are going to decide when to output the special BOSS message.

The overall, outline solution has not changed very much. It still consists of three steps:

1. input
2. process
3. output.

Look back at the code for AskFor:

```
PROCEDURE AskFor(VAR AFnum : INTEGER);

BEGIN
   Write('Please type in a four-digit identification number:');
   ReadLn(AFnum)
END;    {AskFor}
```

The requirements of the new procedure are very similar, except that four single chars need to be input rather than a single four-digit integer. So the new procedure will need four parameters of type char:

```
PROCEDURE AskFor2(VAR AFletter1, AFletter2, AFletter3,
                  AFletter4 : CHAR);
```

Similarly, the ReadLn statement will need to read four chars rather than one integer:

```
ReadLn(AFletter1, AFletter2, AFletter3, AFletter4);
```

The four letters will need to be typed without any spaces between them, as the space is itself a character.

If you type

ABCD   (and then press Enter)

then these four letters will be stored in the variables AFletter1, AFletter2, AFletter3 and AFletter4. But if you type

A □ B □ C □ D   (and then press Enter)

where '□' represents a space, then the variables AFletter1 and AFletter3 will contain A and B, and the variables AFletter2 and AFletter4 will each contain '□' (a space character). The remaining characters C □ D will be disregarded.

The processing will need two procedures. One procedure will check whether all the digits are the same, and so will be very similar to CheckDifferent, except that again the parameter list will include four chars rather than one integer.

The second procedure will need to check whether the first character is 'B', the second character is 'O', and the third and fourth characters are 'S'. You will need to use quote marks around these letters to distinguish 'B' which is 'literally the letter B' from B which could be an identifier for a variable or procedure.

If you wanted to check whether three char variables contained the letters 'C', 'A', 'T', you would need to test

(letter1 = 'C') AND (letter2 ='A') AND (letter3 = 'T').

Char variables are stored using their ASCII code numbers, and so 'A' is not the same as 'a'. Thus the code 'c', 'a', 't' would not pass the above test.

If the code does have all letters the same, there is no need to test again for 'BOSS'. So you will need to include an if statement in the main program to deal with this situation.

The output procedure will need to include three messages for the three cases of

1. a 'BOSS' code;
2. another valid code;
3. an invalid code.

The procedure will need two value parameters of type Boolean; one parameter will contain the result of the all-the-same check, and the other will contain the result of the 'BOSS' check.

EXERCISE 5.11

Step 1. Write new procedures for the input, process and output tasks, and add them to the library unit veribase.pas.

Step 2. Alter your main program so that it can test character codes and report whether they are valid. Save it as verify4.pas.

Step 3. Compile, run and test your program. Don't forget to record your test data, and the predicted and actual output.

EXERCISE 5.12

What happens if you input a four-digit code to this program?

There is a difference between the number 1 and the character '1'. An important difference is that arithmetic can only be performed on numbers, and not on characters. The type 'char' includes any character which can be entered at the keyboard – letters, digits, punctuation and symbols.

EXERCISE 5.13

Step 1. Run the program again, to show that entering digits and punctuation can result in valid codes.

Step 2. Do you think there would be any advantages to reading the original number as a character code rather than an integer?

EXERCISE 5.14

The procedures AskFor and Check will be used again in future case studies.
Copy them both to utils.pas, renaming them AskForPin and CheckPin, and changing parameter and local variable names as appropriate, e.g. AFnum will become AFPnum.
(If you have an earlier version of Turbo Pascal, which only allows one file to be open at a time, you may find it easier to copy via the Windows clipboard or a word processing package.)

EXERCISE 5.15

These exercises are designed to help you to test yourself on the knowledge which you should have acquired in reading this chapter and doing the previous exercises.

1. Explain in your own words why the procedure Check has one parameter which is of type var and one which is a value type parameter.
2. Explain why there are two possible results of integer division, and how these are accessed.
3. Explain what should be included in the interface of a library.
4. Explain what should be included in the implementation section of a library.
5. State the syntax of the two forms of the 'if' structure.
6. Explain what is meant by 'nested ifs'.
7. What is a relational operator?
8. Explain why a programming language should have rules of operator precedence.
9. Describe the values which might be held by the three pervasive types: integer, Boolean and char.
10. What is a logical operator? Give two programming constructions with which it can be used.

6
Statistical package

Before starting this chapter you should be able to do the following:

- use the Pascal environment to edit, compile and run
- design a test plan
- use a unit dependency diagram
- use selection (if) statements and logical operators
- write and use procedures with parameters.

Before tackling this chapter you should have produced a utilities unit containing:

- Welcome
- Farewell
- Pause
- RestoreColour
- AskForPin
- CheckPin.

After tackling this chapter you should understand:

- arithmetic on real numbers
- output formatting
- functions
- relational operators
- case statements.

After tackling this chapter you will have produced a utilities unit containing:

- Welcome
- Farewell
- Pause
- RestoreColour
- AskForPin
- CheckPin
- IsInRange
- AreYouSure.

6.1   Introduction to statistical package

In this case study, you are given a ready-written library which will carry out a number of operations on a list of numbers. You are also given a main program which is designed to use aspects of this library, but also uses some procedures and functions which will have to be written by the user.

statbase.pas is the ready-written unit. In this chapter, you will initially compile this unit, but it is not intended that you will read and understand it. The descriptions of the contents of this library are given for their use.

statprog.pas is the main program, which will use some code which has to be written by you.

statutil.pas will be the unit which you will write; the descriptions of its elements are given.

utils.pas will again be used as in previous case studies.

The program requirements are stated as follows:

The program will allow for the input of a list of real numbers, and will allow the calculation of various statistics from those numbers. These will include the calculation of the range and mean, whether all the numbers are equal, whether they are all positive, whether they are all negative, the sum of the squares, the variance, and the winning margin.

This exercise depends on some knowledge of statistical calculation.

The **total** of a list is determined by adding together all the values.

The **maximum** of a list is the largest value in the list, taking into account the sign.

The **minimum** of a list is the smallest value in the list, taking into account the sign.

The **count** function returns the number of numbers in the list (an integer).

The **second largest** of a list is the value which, after ignoring the largest value, is the largest remaining, taking into account the sign.

The **range** of a list is the difference between the maximum and minimum of a list.

The **mean** of a list is the result of dividing the total of the list by the number of numbers in the list.

The condition '**all are equal**' occurs when every value in the list has the same value.

The condition '**all are positive**' occurs when every value in the list has a value greater than or equal to zero.

The condition '**all are negative**' occurs when every value in the list has a value less than or equal to zero.

The **sum of squares** of a list is obtained by adding together the results of multiplying each number in the list by itself.

The **variance** of a list is obtained by adding together the results of calculating the difference between each number in the list and the mean, squaring each of these values, adding up the total and dividing by the number of numbers in the list.

The **winning margin** of a list is obtained by finding the difference between the maximum in the list and the second largest.

6.2   Real numbers

In previous work, numerical values have all been held as whole numbers only in the variable type known as integer. 'Real' numbers allow for the storage of numbers containing decimal points. Different versions of Pascal will allow for varying degrees of accuracy, but a general rule of thumb is that a real variable is able to hold about ten digits, wherever the decimal point occurs. The technical definition of real numbers for a particular version of Pascal will be given in any manual supplied with that version. No examples in this book go beyond holding about six digits. For more complex arithmetic, a further study of reals is needed, but that is beyond the scope of this book.

In this context, the significant digits of a real number are all those apart from the zeros at either end. Digits other than zero are described as significant because they represent a value, whereas zeros are present simply to indicate the place of other digits within the number.

Real numbers are actually held in two parts, the first being significant digits, and the second a record of where the decimal place goes. The storage areas for each of these, formally called the mantissa and exponent, are limited. A rule of thumb is that the maximum value in the record of where the decimal point goes may be around 38. In other words, numbers which end with about 38 zeros, or which start with about 38 zeros after the decimal point can usually be stored, each with about ten digits of accuracy.

In this book, the most common fractional value to be held in a real variable will be a currency value, and many currencies, such as dollars, pounds and marks are held to two decimal places; that is, there are two significant digits held after the decimal point, so that the value is held to the nearest cent, penny or pfennig.

Real numbers are stored with as much accuracy as possible, but the programmer can choose the accuracy to which they are output. Use of the different forms of output does not alter the underlying stored number. In specifying the output of a real value, two figures are normally given in the WriteLn or Write statement. The first number states the minimum field width; this means the total number of the digits, the sign and the decimal point (if applicable). The second number gives the number of digits to be displayed after the decimal point. (From these two numbers, the other important figure, the number of digits before the decimal point, can be worked out.)

Typical output statements for a real can have . . .

no formatting data, such as `WriteLn(total);`
or one piece of formatting data, such as `WriteLn(result:10);`
or two pieces of formatting data, such as `WriteLn(value:12:4);`

The two items of formatting data could be represented by an integer variable rather than an actual value as shown above. Real numbers are not printed with several zeros on the beginning (known as 'leading zeros') before the decimal point, even if the field width suggests this. Non-significant leading zeros are replaced by spaces, so that numbers less than one have a single zero at the front. Allowance is also made within the rules of output for reals so that a sign can be placed at the beginning. This is either the minus sign ($-$), or a space ($\square$). (Throughout this chapter, when a space is to be represented, to emphasise where it is, the symbol $\square$ is used. In the actual situation, the space symbol $\square$ is used, but, of course, this is not seen in printing.)

The maximum number of decimal places which can be displayed in Turbo Pascal is 11, and if the second value is larger than this, it is treated as if it were 11.

If the field width only is specified, but is not large enough to output all the significant digits stored, the field width given is ignored. If this is the case, enough characters are written to express the value stored. If the field width is not specified, a value of 17 is assumed. If a value of less than 8 is specified, a value of 8 is assumed.

The exponential format is used in two cases. First when the field width is not specified, and secondly where a field width is specified, without a number of decimal places, but the field width is not adequate to represent the number. Exponential form is commonly used in scientific circles. This gives the fractional value, followed by a capital 'E' followed by an 'exponent' or 'power' to represent the multiplication of the first number by ten raised to that power.

In this notation, for example, 2.1234567E+2 represents 212.34567, as the decimal part (the mantissa) should be multiplied by 10^2. In the examples which follow in this book, you will not normally be expected to use this notation. It is mentioned here mainly to reassure you if you discover that output is in a form which you have not seen before. In many of these cases, the simple remedy will be to alter the formatting data in your real output statements, or include it if it has been omitted.

If the number of decimal places is specified, then this is used, and the field width value will be overruled if the decimal form of the number is wider than the field width specified.

A leading space or minus sign always starts a number in exponential format, but a fixed point format may have no leading character.

An example of typical outputs, where: `a=−4.321`, `b=23400000.0`, `c=0.000987`, `d=6`, and `e=2` would be as follows.

Instruction	Output	Explanation
`WriteLn(a:8:3)`	□□−4.321	A total of eight characters are output, with three decimal places; two spaces are placed at the start to fill the full width requested
`WriteLn(b:6:1)`	23400000.0	A total of 10 characters are output, with one decimal place, the field width is overruled. There is no leading space
`WriteLn(c:10:7)`	□0.0009870	A total of 10 characters are output, with seven decimal places; a space is placed at the start to fill the full width requested
`WriteLn(a)`	−4.3210000000E+00	A width of 17 is assumed; exponential notation is assumed
`WriteLn(b:10)`	□2.340E+07	The number of decimal places is not specified, so exponential form is used, with the width of 10 as specified
`WriteLn(c:5)`	□9.9E−04	The number of decimal places is not specified, so exponential form is used, but the width specified is below eight, so eight is assumed. The output answer has been rounded, but the exact value is still stored
`WriteLn(a:25:22)`	□□□□□□□□□□□−4.32100000000	The maximum number of decimal places displayed is 11; the full width of 25 is made up with spaces
`WriteLn(b:d:e)`	23400000.00	The field width specified is too small, so it is ignored; two decimal places are specified. The field width used is the minimum to show the whole number

6.3 Functions

The idea of procedures has been introduced previously and used in some of the case studies. The idea of a function is similar, but has one major difference. Both procedures and functions carry out a series of instructions, but the difference lies in the way the results are returned. Procedures are instructions in their own right and are used as a line of code on their own. Functions produce a result which is calculated as a value by evaluating the function. In other words, a call of a function is used where a value of the type in the function definition could be used. For this reason, a function is only used as part of an instruction, not as a full instruction in itself. In other words, a function produces an answer only, and the program must state what is to be done with the answer produced.

One example of a pervasive function used in this case study is Sqr. This function must be given a single parameter (in the case of functions, a parameter is sometimes called an 'argument'). The result of the function Sqr is to return the square of the input value, that is the value multiplied by itself. The result is a number, so the instruction which uses Sqr must specify an action to be taken with the result.

Examples of the use of Sqr might be:

Pascal instruction	Effect
`WriteLn('The square of 3 is ',Sqr(3));`	Output is: `The square of 3 is 9`
`result := Sqr(myInput);`	Sets a new value in result which is the square of myInput
`variable := Sqr(1) + Sqr(2) + Sqr(3);`	The value of variable becomes 1+4+9, which is 14

Integer variables and real variables are stored in different ways, but it is possible to transfer values between them. The function Round takes a single parameter of type real and returns an integer value, rounded to the nearest whole number.

Pascal instruction	Effect
`result := 4.3;` `WriteLn('Result, rounded, is ',Round(result))`	Output is: `Result, rounded, is 4`
`myInput := -3.7` `intresult := Round(myInput);`	Sets a new value in intresult of -4

With all functions, the type of any parameters must be specified in the function definition, and the type of the result is also specified. In defining our own functions, this will certainly be the case. In the case of a pervasive function, like Sqr, its definition is given in the manual. This definition will normally state the number and type of the parameters and the type of the result. With some pervasive functions, like Sqr, the definition is written in such a way that the type of the result is the same as the type of the parameter, which makes it more flexible to use. Thus there are effectively two definitions of Sqr, such that the result of Sqr on an integer is an integer (as in the examples above), but the result of Sqr on a real is a real.

The function Abs takes a variable or expression and returns the value of the variable or expression with the sign set to positive. In other words, it returns the magnitude of the result, or its absolute value. Abs can be used with variables or expressions of type integer or real.

Pascal instruction	Effect

`result := -4.3;`
`WriteLn('Absolute result is ',`
`         Abs(result):6:2)`
	Output is:
	`Absolute result is □□4.30`

`myInput := -3.4` `absresult := Abs(myInput);`	Sets a new value in absresult of 3.4

A function is defined in a similar way to a procedure, but the closing bracket is followed by the declaration of the type. In theory, it is possible to use var parameters in a function, but this is clearly bad practice. A function is provided within the language to return a single value, and using var parameters can have unexpected side effects. If you want a section of code to return more than one result, then use a procedure. As has already been said, a function must have a type, and in Pascal this can only be a pervasive type (such as real, integer or Boolean). User-defined types cannot be used for the type of a function.

A function declaration takes the following form:

```
FUNCTION name(parameter list) : type;
```

A typical definition, therefore, might be

```
FUNCTION Range(Rlist : statlist) : REAL;
```

The implementation of a function, like that of a procedure, consists of the header followed by declarations local to the function, and then the executable code. In order to return a value from a function, the function title must be allocated a value. The implementation of the above function might therefore be:

```
BEGIN
    Range := Max(Rlist) — Min(Rlist)
END;    {Range}
```

The value assigned to the function is calculated by working out the maximum (a function also defined below) and subtracting the minimum (also defined below). The two functions Max and Min provided produce real results, so their difference is also a real. The type of the variable sent to Range is statlist, which is imported from statbase. This illustrates clearly that any parameter of a user-defined function can be of a user-defined type, but the result must be a pervasive type.

Functions are not limited to the types real and integer, however. It is common to define a function of type Boolean. This will accept one or more parameters and produce a single result, either true or false. Such a function would be useful in determining whether a value or a set of values meets a particular condition.

6.4 Further pervasive procedures and functions

The first form of the procedure Inc takes a single parameter, which must be a variable, and returns the value which comes next after it. Inc cannot be used with a real variable, because there is no 'next' value defined, but the action is clear with integer parameters: one is added to the value. When ordinal types are defined later on, there will be other types with which Inc can be used.

The second form of Inc allows the use of two parameters, which must be of compatible types. It is a more general form of the single-parameter version described earlier. The first parameter must be a variable, and this is increased in value by the expression given as the second parameter. This second parameter can be a variable, or an expression which has to be evaluated, or a literal. In other words,

```
Inc(result);
```

is equivalent to

```
Inc(result, 1);
```

This pervasive procedure illustrates the difference between variable and value parameters. The first parameter in the two-parameter version of Inc must be a variable, which will hold the result. The second parameter is a value, and so can be a literal, an expression, or a variable whose value is used.

The procedure Dec is similar in structure to Inc, but it decreases the value in the variable. It has the two forms described above for Inc.

So:

Procedure	Is equivalent to
Inc(count)	count := count + 1;
Dec(remainder)	remainder := remainder − 1;
Inc(score, 10)	score := score + 10;
Dec(mark, mean)	mark := mark − mean;

The function UpCase must have a parameter of type char, and its result is of type char. The function UpCase operating on a char-type variable, if it is a letter of the alphabet, produces the same alphabetical character in upper case. In other words, it converts letters, irrespective of their case, to upper case. If the character sent is not alphabetic, it remains unaltered by the action of UpCase.

The UpCase function, because it is of type char, is used where you would normally expect to see a char type expression, as in the following example:

```
myReply := UpCase(myReply);
```

myReply is of type char, so is sent as an actual parameter to UpCase. The result of UpCase is of type char, and the := determines that the result of the function should be placed in the variable myReply.

6.5 Relational operators

Relational operators allow you to compare two values to give an answer of true or false. In other words, the result of a relational operator is a Boolean, and for this reason, it is sometimes referred to as a Boolean expression. You have seen previously how Boolean expressions can be combined using logical operators (AND, OR and NOT). These logical operators can also be used to combine relational operators.

There are six main relational operators, as follows:

Operator	Meaning
>	greater than
>=	greater than or equal to
<	less than
<=	less than or equal to
=	equal to
<>	not equal to

These operators can be used to compare the values of two variables, or the relationship of a variable to a literal value. They can be used to compare two values of the same type (real or integer), and in many cases types can be mixed, such as comparing a real variable with an integer value.

Examples of the use of a relational operator are:

```
FUNCTION AreAllEqual(AAElist : statlist) : BOOLEAN;

BEGIN
   IF Max(AAElist) = Min(AAElist) THEN
   BEGIN
      AreAllEqual := TRUE
   END
   ELSE
   BEGIN
      AreAllEqual := FALSE
   END
END; {AreAllEqual}
```

In this function, the condition Max(AAElist) = Min(AAElist) is either true or false, and the two different branches within the 'if' statement are taken depending on its value. If the values returned by each of the two functions are exactly equal, then the expression is true; in every other case it is false.

```
FUNCTION AreAllPositive(AAPlist : statlist) : BOOLEAN;

BEGIN
   IF Min(AAPlist) >= 0 THEN
   BEGIN
      AreAllPositive := TRUE
   END
   ELSE
   BEGIN
      AreAllPositive := FALSE
   END
END;    {AreAllPositive}
```

In this function, the condition Min(AAPlist) >= 0 is either true or false, and the two different branches within the 'if' statement are taken depending on its value. If the value of the expression is either greater than zero, or exactly equal to it, then the whole condition is true. If this is not the case (in other words the value returned by the function is less than zero), then the whole condition is false.

Another example of the use of a relational operator is in the control of a while loop. For example, the repetition of a series of instructions could be controlled by a statement such as:

```
WHILE choice <> 0 DO
```

At times there may be a more complex condition, such as the following statement, in which the exit condition is that a variable takes one of two possible answers, or the loop has been executed a stated number of times.

```
WHILE (lAYSreply <> 'Y') AND (lAYSreply <> 'N')
        AND (lAYScount <= AYSlimit) DO
```

This construction is common because a user may never give an acceptable response, and it is important not to allow a program to loop forever.

A further use of a relational operator is to assign a value to a Boolean variable. A statement such as this looks initially rather peculiar, but is a good illustration of the difference between the symbol for the assignment statement (:=) and the relational operator (=). The assignment statement is often read as 'becomes equal to', whereas the relational operator is referred to as 'is equal to'.

A shorter, alternative, version of AreAllPositive using this syntax would be:

```
FUNCTION AreAllPositive(AAPlist : statlist) : BOOLEAN;

BEGIN
    AreAllPositive := Min(AAPlist) >= 0
END;    {AreAllPositive}
```

6.6   The scope of variables

One very important aspect of the design of Pascal is its emphasis on the scope of a variable. The scope is the term used to describe those parts of the program or unit in which a variable can be accessed. If an attempt is made to access a variable outside its scope, an error message will be produced by the compiler.

Throughout this book, you have begun to be used to seeing a very formal convention for giving parameters and variables names, usually referred to as identifiers. This has been done in an attempt to emphasise good design from the start. You will read in all the Pascal manuals and many of the Pascal books that there are, in fact, very few restrictions on what variables or parameters may be called. The convention that has been used in this book minimises the chances of the same name being used twice or more.

If you were to be less rigid than you have been shown in this book about your choice of names, you would find that in most cases the programs and units would function just as well. However, the naming convention used here is an attempt to emphasise the scope of various declarations.

The declaration of a parameter in a procedure or function definition allows the parameter to be referred to in the procedure or function for which it is declared. The convention used in this book has suggested that the name of parameters should begin with initial capitals of the procedure or function for which it is declared. This helps avoid ambiguity, and also emphasises, by contrast, those identifiers which are not parameters.

Where variables are declared within a procedure or function, using a 'var' declaration, these identifiers are said to be local to the procedure or function. This means that they cannot be accessed outside the procedure or function. In other words, these identifiers have limited scope. The convention used in this book is that local identifiers begin with a lower case l followed by the initial letters of the procedure or function to which they are local. Local variables are sometimes described as 'mortal' because they are considered to have a life only when the procedure or function is invoked or called, and that the values are lost or killed off when the task of the procedure or function is completed.

It follows from this consideration of the scope of identifiers that, within a procedure or function, the only identifiers which are normally used are the parameters of the procedure or function and constants and variables local to the procedure or function. The convention used in this book makes it relatively easy to check that each procedure or function refers only to parameters or local variables.

It also follows, in checking for good style in coding, that all the parameters and local variables which are declared in a procedure or function should be referred to within its implementation. If this is not the case, then data is being prepared or stored and not used. This will almost always indicate a poor design or a lack of 'tidying up' of code when alterations have been made.

6.7 Describing the design

In this case study, all the decisions have been made for you about which aspects go in which units. The data structure, procedures and functions are provided in statbase. The main program is given in a complete form. The gap, which is represented by the functions and procedures used by the main program but which are not in statbase, must be filled by your own procedures and functions which will be in statutil.

The main program is provided as follows:

```
PROGRAM statprog;
{
    Main program for Chapter 6 - Statistics
    Reads in a list of numbers and then displays various
    statistics about the list
    Written by AMC/MPW
    1:1:96
}

USES statbase, statutil, utils;

VAR usercode : INTEGER;
    isvalid  : BOOLEAN;
    data     : statlist;

BEGIN
    RestoreColour;
    Welcome;
    AskForPin(usercode);
    CheckPin(usercode, isvalid);
    IF isvalid THEN
    BEGIN
        EnterData(data);
        WriteLn('The range is ',Range(data):12:4);
        WriteLn('The mean is ',Mean(data):12:4);
        IF AreAllEqual(data) THEN
        BEGIN
            WriteLn('Numbers are all equal')
        END
        ELSE
        BEGIN
            WriteLn('Numbers are not all equal')
```

```
      END;     {IF}
      IF AreAllPositive(data) THEN
      BEGIN
         WriteLn('Numbers are all positive')
      END
      ELSE
      BEGIN
         WriteLn('Numbers are not all positive')
      END;     {IF}
      IF AreAllNegative(data) THEN
      BEGIN
         WriteLn('Numbers are all negative')
      END
      ELSE
      BEGIN
         WriteLn('Numbers are not all negative')
      END;     {IF}
      WriteLn('The sum of squares is ',SumOfSquares(data):12:4);
      WriteLn('The variance is ',Variance(data):12:4);
      WriteLn('The winning margin is ',WinningMargin(data):12:4);
   END
   ELSE
   BEGIN
      WriteLn('Sorry, you can only use this program with a correct
               code')
   END;     {IF}
   Pause;
   Farewell;
   RestoreColour
END.     {statprog}
```

The data structure statlist is defined within statbase, and is capable of holding a list of numbers, and of knowing how many are in the list. As the unit is provided, it is capable of holding a list with a maximum size of 10. With access to the source code of statbase, however, this could be suitably amended.

The relevant part of the interface section of statbase is given here so that the reader understands what is provided:

```
PROCEDURE EnterData(VAR EDlist : statlist);
{
      Pre-condition:    none
      Action:           accepts the input of the number of numbers in
                        the list, followed by the stated number of
                        numbers (as reals)
      Post-condition:   returns input data, the list and its size, in
                        data structure of type statlist, whose
                        implementation is hidden
}
PROCEDURE DisplayData(DDlist : statlist);
{
      Pre-condition:    is sent a valid list of data in a statlist
```

```
        Action:              displays numbers in the list
        Post-condition:      none
}
FUNCTION Total(Tlist : statlist) : REAL;
{
        Pre-condition:       is sent a valid list of data in a statlist
        Action:              calculates sum of all values in the list
        Post-condition:      returns sum of values as function value
}
FUNCTION Max(Mlist : statlist) : REAL;
{
        Pre-condition:       is sent a valid list of data in a statlist
        Action:              calculates largest of all values in the list
        Post-condition:      returns largest of values as function value
}
FUNCTION Min(Mlist : statlist) : REAL;
{
        Pre-condition:       is sent a valid list of data in a statlist
        Action:              calculates smallest of all values in the list
        Post-condition:      returns smallest of values as function value
}
FUNCTION Count(Clist : statlist) : INTEGER;
{
        Pre-condition:       is sent a valid list of data in a statlist
        Action:              counts the number of numbers in the list
        Post-condition:      returns number of numbers as function value
}
FUNCTION SecondLargest(SLlist : statlist) : REAL;
{
        Pre-condition:       is sent a valid list of data in a statlist
        Action:              calculates largest value in the remainder of
                             the list when the largest value is ignored
        Post-condition:      returns second largest of values as function
                             value
}
PROCEDURE ReduceListBy(VAR RLBlist : statlist; RLBvalue : REAL);
{
        Pre-condition:       is sent a valid list of data in a statlist as
                             the first parameter, and a real value as the
                             second parameter
        Action:              generates a new list of values in which each
                             entry has a value given by subtracting the
                             second parameter from the corresponding value
                             in the original list
        Post-condition:      returns updated list of values as first
                             parameter, as described above; the second
                             parameter is unaltered
}
PROCEDURE Square(VAR Slist : statlist);
{
        Pre-condition:       is sent a valid list of data in a statlist as
                             the parameter
```

```
        Action:              generates a new list of values in which each
                             entry has a value given by multiplying the
                             corresponding value in the original list by
                             itself
        Post-condition:      returns updated list of values as parameter,
                             as described above
}
PROCEDURE CopyList(CLlist1 : statlist; VAR CLlist2 : statlist);
{
        Pre-condition:       is sent a valid list of data in a statlist as
                             the first parameter
        Action:              generates a new list of values in which each
                             entry has the same value as the corresponding
                             value in the original list
        Post-condition:      returns updated list of values as second
                             parameter, as described above; the original
                             list is unaltered
}
```

From this information, it is clear that the following functions are not provided, and must be written by the reader:

- Range
- Mean
- AreAllEqual
- AreAllPositive
- AreAllNegative
- SumOfSquares
- Variance
- WinningMargin.

Each of these functions will process a list in the form 'statlist' and produce a single answer. In some cases this will be a real result, in other cases, it will be a Boolean value.

EXERCISE 6.1

In order that you can see an example of the finished product which you should be aiming for in this exercise, a working version, called sstats.exe is provided, in compiled form only.

Step 1. For each of the functions listed above as being in statutil, decide which procedures and functions of statbase will be necessary in order to work out the values required.

Step 2. Draw the unit dependency diagram for the program supplied and the various units it will use.

Step 3. Write the file statutil, which will contain your new functions, compile it and run the main program.

Step 4. Test your new library through using the main program provided.

6.8 The 'case' statement

The 'case' statement allows for a choice with more than two options. The 'if' statement introduced in Chapter 5 allows for a two-way choice, based on any condition which can be expressed as a Boolean expression. The case statement is more limited, in that it can be based only on the value of a variable, but is more general than an 'if' statement because it can allow for many different values with a multiple choice of actions.

The case statement begins with the word case, followed by an identifier (the selector), which is a variable name. After the word 'of', there should be a list of possible actions. This list of actions consists of one or more possible values for the variable, followed by a colon (:), then a statement or a group of statements giving the action to be taken if the variable has those values. According to the convention used in this book, the actions within each branch of the case statement will be enclosed within a 'begin' and 'end', though this is not strictly necessary when there is only one statement in a branch. After the list of possible actions comes the word 'end'. In later examples you will also see the use of the 'else' clause before the 'end'.

Consider this example:

```
CASE choice OF
    1:  BEGIN
            EnterData(data)
        END;
    2:  BEGIN
            WriteLn('The range is ',Range(data):12:4)
        END;
    3:  BEGIN
            WriteLn('The mean is ',Mean(data):12:4)
        END
END;    {CASE}
```

This is a three-way choice of action. If the value in the variable 'choice' is 1, then the action

```
EnterData(data)
```

will be carried out.
    If 'choice' is 2, then the instruction

```
WriteLn('The range is ',Range(data):12:4)
```

is carried out.
    If it is 3, the instruction

```
WriteLn('The mean is ',Mean(data):12:4)
```

is executed.
    In all other cases, that is when choice is none of the values 1, 2 or 3, then no action is carried out.

Notice that this is an example where an 'end' is used which has not had a previous matching 'begin'. This can be considered unfortunate, as many programmers like to check their programs by matching the 'begin' and 'end' statements. In terms of indentation according to the convention used in this book, a case statement is treated as equivalent to a 'begin', so indentation starts immediately after it.

Case statements can use other variable types, though it would be unusual to use a Boolean, as an 'if' statement would be more appropriate in that case. Reals cannot be used in case statements, as the values have to match exactly, and there is too much scope for rounding errors. Variables of type char are also frequently used in case statements.

The values in the case label can be in the form of a list, separated by commas. Such a list will be followed after the colon by the action to be taken if any of those values is taken by the selector.

Another possible form of entry in the case label is a subrange. This is used to indicate that all the values in a specified range are allowed. For example the notation

2..6

indicates all values from

2 to 6

and is equivalent to

2, 3, 4, 5, 6

Subranges can be included with single values or other subranges in a list in a case label, such as:

4..20,   24..30

which are all the days of the month where the day number is pronounced with 'th' on the end

1,   21,   31

are all the days pronounced with a 'st'
and

2,   22

are all the days pronounced with 'nd'
and

3,   23

are all the days pronounced with 'rd'

The 'else' section of the 'case' statement is part of Turbo Pascal which is an extension to standard Pascal. A list of possible values is followed by an 'else' clause, which is the word 'else' followed by an action. This action will be carried out if the variable does not match any of the values suggested. Rather like the 'if . . . then . . . else' construction, this will mean that in every case, precisely one of the alternative actions will be taken.

```
CASE letterchoice OF
      'a', 'A' :  BEGIN
                     WriteLn('You have chosen to enter some data');
                     EnterData(data)
                  END;
      'b', 'B' :  BEGIN
                     WriteLn('The range is ',Range(data):12:4)
                  END;
```

```
      'c',  'C'  :   BEGIN
                       WriteLn('The mean is ',Mean(data):12:4)
                     END;
         ELSE        BEGIN
                       WriteLn('You have chosen to exit')
                     END
END;    {of CASE}
```

In this example, which is another variation on the code which is to be used in our main program, letterchoice is a variable of char type. If the letter 'a' is chosen, either in upper or lower case, then the two statements shown are executed, namely displaying the message about entering data and then the call of the procedure. On the other branches, irrespective of the case of the letters, 'b' and 'c' trigger the other options. In this particular example, any other choices of character will lead to the display of the message 'You have chosen to exit', and no other action. This would not lead to a particularly user-friendly program, but is shown here to illustrate the principles.

EXERCISE 6.2

Step 1. Design and write a Boolean function, for inclusion in utils, with the following specification

```
FUNCTION AreYouSure(AYSlimit: INTEGER) : BOOLEAN;
{
   Pre-condition:      parameter contains the number of attempts the
                       user will be allowed to input a correct choice;
                       it must be greater than zero
   Action:             asks user whether he/she is sure, and accepts
                       an input; if the reply is 'Y', 'y', 'N' or 'n',
                       then a result is returned, otherwise the ques-
                       tion is asked again and a further input is
                       waited for; if, after the number of specified
                       attempts has been used, an answer of neither
                       'yes' nor 'no' has been received, then the
                       answer 'no' is assumed
   Post-condition:     result is TRUE if a valid reply is received and
                       it is 'Y' or 'y'; result is FALSE in all other
                       circumstances
}
```

(Hint: The condition for continuing the loop is a compound one as it involves a decision based both on the latest input and on the number of previous goes. Looping will therefore need to be controlled by a while loop with a compound condition combined through an 'and'.)

Step 2. You are given a program statp2, which is a menu-driven program providing some statistical analysis. It is capable of producing the statistics for a list of numbers, and then can be given a new list of numbers to be processed, and then another list if required, and so on, until the user asks to exit the program.

```
PROGRAM statp2;
{
   Second main program for Chapter 6 - Statistics
```

```
      Reads in and processes several different lists
      Written by AMC/MPW
      1:1:96
}

USES statbase, statutil, utils;

VAR usercode, choice : INTEGER;
    isvalid : BOOLEAN;
    data : statlist;

BEGIN
   RestoreColour;
   Welcome;
   AskForPin(usercode);
   CheckPin(usercode, isvalid);
   IF isvalid THEN
   BEGIN
      choice := 10;
      WHILE choice <> 0 DO
      BEGIN
         Menu; {a procedure which the reader will have to write in
                statutil which displays a menu of the choices
                offered below}
         ReadLn(choice);
         CASE choice OF
         1: BEGIN
               EnterData(data)
            END;    {CASE 1}
         2: BEGIN
               WriteLn('The range is ',Range(data):12:4)
            END;    {CASE 2}
         3: BEGIN
               WriteLn('The mean is ',Mean(data):12:4)
            END;    {CASE 3}
         0: BEGIN
               WriteLn('You are about to exit');
               IF NOT AreYouSure(3) THEN
               BEGIN
                  choice := 10
               END
            END    {CASE 0}
         END;    {of CASE}
      END;    {of WHILE}
   END    {of IF}
   ELSE
   BEGIN
      WriteLn('Sorry, you cannot use this program without ');
      WriteLn('the correct code')
   END;
   Pause;
   Farewell;
   RestoreColour
END.   {of statp2}
```

Add extra items to the menu so that all nine functions referred to by statprog can be accessed through the new menu-driven version.

Test this program thoroughly to see if there are any flaws in it. There is a major error built in at the moment.

Step 3. There is a problem with the program produced above if any statistics are asked for without data having been entered. By using a Boolean variable within your main program, keep a record of whether data has been entered, and using 'if' statements, display an error message if features are requested before data is entered.

Step 4. Design and write a Boolean function, for inclusion in utils with the following specification:

```
FUNCTION IsInRange(IIRvalue, IIRmin, IIRmax : INTEGER) : BOOLEAN;
{
    Pre-condition:       all three values are valid integers
    Action:              determines whether the first parameter value
                         is in the range bounded at the lower end by
                         second parameter and at the upper end by
                         third parameter with the boundary values
                         considered to be included in the range
    Post-condition:      result is TRUE if condition applies
}
```

Use this function in your main program to decide to display an error message if the choice is out of the required range.

Step 5. Extend the principle in Step 3 above so that a warning message is displayed if the user attempts to quit the program before any data has been entered.

Step 6. Expand the system by including on the menu any other statistical calculations you can discover, including the ones which are ready-written in statbase.

Step 7. Write a test plan for your new, expanded system, and use it to produce a test log.

Step 8. Draw the unit dependency diagram for your system.

EXERCISE 6.3

Convert the program so that the menu uses alphabetic characters rather than numbers. Choose meaningful letters (such as 'v' for variance), allowing for input in either upper or lower case. Test it thoroughly.

EXERCISE 6.4

Step 1. Write a program which illustrates the eight examples given in the table earlier for formatting of real numbers in the WriteLn instruction. Adapt the program with your own examples.

Step 2. The standard deviation of a set of numbers is the square root of its variance. The pervasive function Sqrt takes a single parameter and returns the positive square root of the parameter. Use this function to add the calculation of the standard deviation to one of your previous programs.

Step 3. Experiment with the use of the Sqrt function to discover the types of parameter which can be used, and the type of the result (that is the function type) in each case. Explain why this happens.

EXERCISE 6.5

These exercises are designed to help you test yourself on the knowledge which you should have acquired in reading this chapter and doing the previous exercises.

1. Write down a list of possible types for a function.
2. Distinguish pervasive functions, functions in a pre-defined unit and user-defined functions. Give two examples of each kind.
3. Explain why the procedure CopyList has one value and one variable parameter.
4. Write a list of pervasive functions used in this chapter.
5. Which function in statbase is of type integer? Explain why.
6. Explain the two contexts in which the word 'else' is used.
7. Explain why the type of the WinningMargin function is the same as the type of the two functions which it uses.
8. What form of a case statement is equivalent to an 'if' statement? Illustrate your answer with an example.
9. Can the function AreYouSure in utils be used with a variable parameter?
10. Why are var parameters unsuitable for use in a function?

7
Dates

Before starting this chapter you should be able to do the following:

- use the Pascal environment to edit, compile and run
- design a test plan
- use a unit dependency diagram
- use selection statements
- write and use procedures and functions with parameters
- carry out arithmetic on integer and real numbers
- format output
- use indefinite (while) loops.

Before tackling this chapter you should have produced a utilities unit containing the following functions and procedures:

- Welcome
- Farewell
- Pause
- RestoreColour
- AskForPin
- CheckPin
- IsInRange
- AreYouSure.

After tackling this chapter you should understand:

- subrange types
- record declarations and their use
- definite loops.

After tackling this chapter, you will have produced a utilities unit containing the following functions and procedures:

- Welcome
- Farewell
- Pause
- RestoreColour

- AskForPin
- CheckPin
- IsInRange
- AreYouSure
- Display4Menu.

7.1   Introduction to date handling

In this chapter, you will work on a program which will process information about dates in the calendar for the year 2001. This year marks the start of the new millennium, and so its dates are perhaps particularly interesting.

In later versions of the program, you will be able to change the year number, as the year is included as a constant in one of the libraries.

You are given a ready-written unit which will define the storage type for and carry out a number of operations on a date. You are also given a main program which is designed to use aspects of this unit. You are initially given a working set of files to compile and run. You will later reuse and adapt the code contained in them.

The program requirements are stated as follows:

The program will allow for the input of a date in the pre-determined year by the entry of a day number and a month number. A four-part menu will then be displayed. The first choice displays a message which states whether the input date is a valid one (so, 28 and 2 is valid, but 32 and 3 is invalid because there is no such day in March). The second choice displays a message stating which day of the week the input date falls on (though in the first version the validity of the date will not be checked). The third choice displays a message stating which day of the year the input date is (though in the first version the validity of the date will not be checked). The day of the year is defined, for valid dates, as the number of days elapsed in the year so far including the current day, so 1st January is 1, 5th February is 36 and so on. The fourth menu option provides a means of exit.

For the first working program the possible messages to be displayed are as follows:

	Message	Use of message
1	That is not a valid menu choice	Displayed when a menu selection is made which is out of the required range
2	You have chosen to exit	Displayed when the exit option is chosen from the menu
3	Please input the day number in the range 1 to 31	Displayed when the first part of a date input is being requested
4	and the month in the range 1 to 12	Displayed when the second part of a date input is being requested
5	1. Date exists 2. Day of Week 3. Day of Year 4. Exit	Displayed as main menu, after a possible date (both elements) has been input
6	That is a valid date in xxxx (where xxxx is a year number)	Displayed when the date input is a date in the given year
7	That is not a valid date in xxxx (where xxxx is a year number)	Displayed when the date input is not a date in the given year

	Message	Use of message
8	That date will fall on a xxxday in xxxx (where xxxday represents a day, and xxxx is a year number)	Displayed (when 2 is chosen from menu) to state on which day of the week the input day falls in the given year
9	That date is day number xxx in xxxx (where xxx represents a day number in the year (between 1 and 366), and xxxx is a year number)	Displayed (when 3 is chosen from menu) to state on which day of the year the input day falls in the given year
10	Are you sure (Y/N)?	Displayed (as part of function in utils) when exit option has been chosen
11	Sorry, you have exhausted the maximum number of goes	Displayed (as part of function in utils) when exit option has been chosen
12	Sorry, that is not a valid choice, please try again	Displayed (as part of function in utils) when exit option has been chosen
13	Press ENTER to continue	Displayed (as part of Pause procedure in utils) when messages are being displayed
14	Welcome	Displayed (as part of Welcome procedure in utils)
15	Farewell	Displayed (as part of Farewell procedure in utils) when exit option has been chosen, though can be replaced by any other message

The files which are provided in the directory chap7 are as follows:

- datebase.pas is the ready-written unit; initially, you will be using the contents of this unit from the descriptions given; later in the chapter it will be explained how they work;
- dateprog.pas is the main program;
- dateutil.pas is the unit which you will write; the descriptions of its elements are given, along with dummy versions of the procedures in it;
- utils.pas from the previous chapters will be required, and will, as part of one of the exercises, have an extra procedure added, which is initially provided as forutils.pas;
- forutils.pas which contains a new procedure that will be added to utils later.

EXERCISE 7.1

Step 1. Using the four pas files provided, and your current utils from the last chapter, compile them in the following order:

- datebase
- forutils
- utils
- dateutil
- dateprog.

Run the program. Write down what the program does, and explain how this falls short of the specification given above.

Step 2. By running the program, determine what will happen if:

(a) a date which exists is input under option 1;
(b) a date which exists is input under option 2;
(c) a date which exists is input under option 3;
(d) a date which does not exist is input under option 1;
(e) a date which does not exist is input under option 2;
(f) a date which does not exist is input under option 3.

Step 3. Print a listing of the main program. Underline the Pascal reserved words in red. Indicate by using different colours or notations where all identifiers are defined.

Step 4. Introduce the use of AskForPin and CheckPin at the start of the program to restrict access to those who know the code.

The code provided falls short of the requirement in a number of ways. Messages 6, 7, 8 and 9 in the table of messages are not output in the desired form. You should be able to see, however, from what is output, that the procedures which should output the correct messages have access to the information which they need. One of your first tasks in the next set of exercises will be to replace the procedures outputting these replies, all of which are in dateutil.

In order to work on these files further, it is appropriate that you now examine their content and their relationship.

The main program looks like this:

```
PROGRAM dateprog;
{
    Main program for Chapter 7 - Dates
    provides options to enter date, to display whether a date is
    valid and to display the day of the week and the day of the year
    Written by AMC/MPW
       1:1:96
}
USES dateutil, database, utils, forutils, crt;

VAR   dayno       : DayOfYearType;
      daywk       : DayOfWeekType;
      indate      : DateType;
      choice      : MenuChoiceType;

BEGIN
    Welcome;
    choice := 0;
    WHILE choice <> 4 DO
    BEGIN
        ClrScr;
        ReadDate(indate);
        AcceptMenuChoice(choice);
        IF IsInRange(choice, 1, 4) THEN
        BEGIN
```

```
         CASE choice OF
         1: BEGIN
               WriteMessage(IsValidDate(indate))
            END;    {of CASE 1}
         2: BEGIN
               WriteDayOfWeek(CalculatedDayOfWeek(indate))
            END;    {of CASE 2}
         3: BEGIN
               WriteDayOfYear(CalculatedDayOfYear(indate))
            END;    {of CASE 3}
         4: BEGIN
               WriteLn('You have chosen to exit');
               IF NOT AreYouSure(3) THEN
               BEGIN
                  choice := 0
               END    {IF}
            END    {of CASE 4}
         END    {CASE}
      END    {first part of IF}
      ELSE
      BEGIN
         WriteLn('That is not a valid menu choice')
      END;    {of IF}
      Pause
   END;    {WHILE}
   Farewell
END.   {dateprog}
```

This program almost conforms to the typical pattern you have seen so far in the relationship of the units. The units database and dateutil are specially written for this chapter. As usual, database can be used without understanding how each of the elements in it work, though later in this chapter it will be explained in full. The unit utils, the utilities unit which is developed chapter by chapter, is again used. One extra unit, called forutils, is provided separately. Its contents can be later moved into utils to restore the usual pattern of the four units. Also, as normal, you will call on procedures in crt.

The program dateprog contains a main loop (WHILE choice <> 4 DO) which allows the user to carry out the task of converting a date several times, terminating the process by entering 4 on the menu. Within the loop, there is an 'if' statement, which allows the correct action to be carried out if a valid choice is made from the menu, or displays a message if the choice was not valid.

The interface section of database appears as follows:

```
CONST thisyear = 2001;

TYPE DayOfWeekType = 1..7;
     DayOfMonthType = 0..31;
     DayOfYearType = 1..366;
     MonthType = 1..12;
     YearType = 1901..2099;
```

```
        DateType = RECORD
                     DayofWeek   : DayOfWeekType;
                     Day         : DayOfMonthType;
                     Month       : MonthType;
                     Year        : YearType
        END   {RECORD};

 FUNCTION DaysInMonth(DIMmonth : MonthType) : DayOfMonthType;
 {
        Pre-condition:    is sent data in a MonthType as the parameter
        Action:           determines the number of days in the month
                          given
        Post-condition:   returns DayOfMonthType value containing the
                          number of days
 }
 FUNCTION IsValidDate(IVDdate : DateType) : BOOLEAN;
 {
        Pre-condition:    is sent data in a DateType as the parameter
        Action:           determines whether the date given is a valid
                          date
        Post-condition:   returns Boolean value containing TRUE if the
                          date is a valid one, and FALSE otherwise
 }
 FUNCTION CalculatedDayOfYear(CDOYdate : DateType) : DayOfYearType;
 {
        Pre-condition:    is sent data in a DateType as the parameter
        Action:           determines the day of the year of the given
                          date; for valid dates this is defined as the
                          number of days up to the given day of the
                          year; for invalid dates, the value is undefined
        Post-condition:   returns DayOfYearType value containing the day
                          number within the year
 }
 FUNCTION CalculatedDayOfWeek(CDOWdate : DateType) : DayOfWeekType;
 {
        Pre-condition:    is sent data in a DateType as the parameter
        Action:           determines the day of the week of the given
                          date; for valid dates this is defined as 1 for
                          Sunday, 2 for Monday, ... 7 for Saturday; for
                          invalid dates, the value is undefined
        Post-condition:   returns a DayOfWeekType value containing the
                          day number within the week
 }
```

7.2 Type declarations, subrange types and record types

In the interface of datebase, there are a number of type declarations. These allow you to establish variables of types different from those which are pervasive. You should already be familiar with a number of pervasive types, which are integer, real, char and Boolean. In this chapter, you will see two methods for declaring your own type, which is usually referred to as a user-defined type.

In-built in any language like Pascal, there are a number of types, which may be used on their own or may be used as the basic building blocks for other types.

Declarations such as

```
DayOfWeekType = 1..7;
```

establish a new type, called a subrange type, which can then be used either in a variable declaration or as a type for a parameter of a procedure or function. In fact, subrange types of pervasive types can be used wherever a pervasive type can be used. The declaration of DayOfWeekType above specifies that any variable of type DayOfWeekType can have a value in the range 1 to 7. From this information, the compiler will infer the other possible values in the range. It does this by acknowledging that the values 1 and 7 are those normally taken by an integer type. This relationship is important, because this also means that any operation which can be carried out on an integer can be carried out on a DayOfWeekType. If this were not the case, you would have to declare every operation which can be carried out on a DayOfWeekType.

In a similar way, the declaration

```
DayOfMonthType = 0..31;
```

establishes a type which can take values in the range 0 to 31. Three other declarations in datebase work in the same way.

These various subrange types can be accessed in any of the other units which have been declared to use datebase. The pattern in this chapter is typical of the hierarchy of units. The unit database is used by various other units and the main program, and its types are used by those various other files.

The other type declaration in datebase specifies the type DateType.

```
DateType =  RECORD
               DayofWeek  : DayOfWeekType;
               Day        : DayOfMonthType;
               Month      : MonthType;
               Year       : YearType
    END    {RECORD};
```

This is a declaration of a record type, which is an example of a structured type. Record types consist of several components, or fields, which can be of different types. Each field is given an identifier and a type. A variable of a record type can be manipulated as a whole record in, for example, an assignment statement or as a parameter for a procedure. Alternatively, individual fields can be accessed by referring to a field name qualified by a variable of the record type. This means that the variable name is followed by a full stop and the field name; such an expression has the type of the named field.

The declaration of DateType states that each variable of type DateType is a record which contains four fields. In this particular case, they all happen to be user-defined types, but they could equally well use some pervasive types.

The procedure ReadDate in dateutil has a parameter, RDdate, of type DateType. The procedure handles the parts, or fields, of RDdate separately. Look at the code of the implementation of ReadDate:

```
PROCEDURE ReadDate(VAR RDdate : DateType);

BEGIN
    ReadDayNo(RDdate.Day);
    ReadMonth(RDdate.Month);
    RDdate.Year := thisyear
END;    {ReadDate}
```

This procedure calls two other procedures that are local to dateutil. This means that they are declared in the implementation, but are not declared in the interface. Therefore they can be used by procedures in dateutil but cannot be accessed outside by any program or unit that uses dateutil. As local procedures must, by definition, be used by other procedures that are in that unit (in this case dateutil), they would have to be declared before them, in order that the unit will compile properly. It is therefore normal to put the local procedures at the start of the implementation of a unit.

```
PROCEDURE ReadDayNo(VAR RDNday : DayOfMonthType);
BEGIN
    WriteLn('Please input the day number in the range 1 to 31');
    ReadLn(RDNday)
END;

PROCEDURE ReadMonth(VAR RMmonth : MonthType);
BEGIN
    WriteLn('and the month in the range 1 to 12');
    ReadLn(RMmonth)
END;
```

Fields of RDdate are addressed three times in ReadDate. In each case, the name of the variable (RDdate) is followed by a dot, then a field name. In this case, RDdate.Day is of type DayOfMonthType, and so a ReadDayOfMonth can be carried out on it. Similarly, RDdate.Month is of type MonthType. RDdate.Year is of type YearType.

Notice, in this case, that the value of one of the fields of RDdate, DayOfWeek, is not set. This, though unusual, is quite acceptable, as long as the value in this field is not used, as its value is not defined, and cannot be predicted. This field has been included here so that the data structure is consistent with the development of the later date work in Chapter 9.

In this case study, the day of the week is calculated by the function CalculatedDayOfWeek and is returned as the result of the function. The result is then immediately used for output. The field DayOfWeek in the date is not set because while CalculatedDayOfWeek could alter this field with the parameter set as a variable parameter, the use of a variable parameter in a function is bad practice. Since the DayOfWeek is used only once, the setting of the field is not necessary.

7.3 Understanding the code provided

In the interface of datebase, there is a declaration

```
CONST thisyear = 2001;
```

This is the part which declares the year used throughout the chapter, which needs to be accessed by other units. In later exercises, you will input year numbers rather than use this constant so that your program will function for a different year.

The file dateutil contains the correct descriptions of what each procedure should do, and appears as follows:

```
UNIT dateutil;

INTERFACE

USES datebase, forutils;

TYPE MenuChoiceType = 0..4;

PROCEDURE ReadDate(VAR RDdate : DateType);
{
    Pre-condition:      none
    Action:             accepts the day number element of a date in
                        response to the message 'Please input the
                        day number in the range 1 to 31', and the
                        month number element of a date in response
                        to the message, 'and the month in the range
                        1 to 12'
    Post-condition:     returns input data in data structure of type
                        DateType, with year set to value held in
                        constant thisyear
}
PROCEDURE AcceptMenuChoice(VAR AMCinput : MenuChoiceType);
{
    Pre-condition:      none
    Action:             displays menu of options and accepts a
                        response
    Post-condition:     returns input data
}
PROCEDURE WriteMessage(WManswer : BOOLEAN);
{
    Pre-condition:      is sent a BOOLEAN value
    Action:             displays either 'Date is valid' or 'Date is
                        not valid' message, depending on value passed
                        in as parameter
    Post-condition:     none
}
PROCEDURE WriteDayOfWeek(WDOWday : DayOfWeekType);
{
    Pre-condition:      is sent a parameter of type DayOfWeekType
    Action:             displays day of the week indicated by value
                        it is sent with 1 representing Sunday, 2
                        representing Monday and so on
    Post-condition:     none
}
```

```
PROCEDURE WriteDayOfYear(WDOYday : DayOfYearType);
{
      Pre-condition:      is sent a parameter of type DayOfYearType
      Action:             displays day of the year indicated by value
                          it is sent
      Post-condition:     none
}
```

The version of dateutil supplied includes dummy versions of the procedures. These work in an elementary way, but will have to be altered. In this dummy form, you have compiled and run the program to ensure that all the components are present and that the program control is correct. You will later replace the procedures with their proper versions.

The procedure AcceptMenuChoice uses a procedure which is provided in forutils, called Display4Menu. The way in which this procedure works is explained later.

```
IMPLEMENTATION

PROCEDURE ReadDayNo(VAR RDNday : DayOfMonthType);

BEGIN
   WriteLn('Please input the day number in the range 1 to 31');
   ReadLn(RDNday)
END;

PROCEDURE ReadMonth(VAR RMmonth : MonthType);

BEGIN
   WriteLn('and the month in the range 1 to 12');
   ReadLn(RMmonth)
END;

PROCEDURE ReadDate(VAR RDdate : DateType);

BEGIN
   ReadDayNo(RDdate.Day);
   ReadMonth(RDdate.Month);
   RDdate.Year := thisyear
END;    {ReadDate}

PROCEDURE AcceptMenuChoice(VAR AMCinput : MenuChoiceType);

BEGIN
   Display4Menu('Date exists', 'Day of Week', 'Day of Year',
   'Exit');
   ReadLn(AMCinput)
END;    {AcceptMenuChoice}

PROCEDURE WriteMessage(WManswer : BOOLEAN);

BEGIN
   WriteLn('Message output will reflect Boolean value')
END;    {WriteMessage}
```

```
PROCEDURE WriteDayOfWeek(WDOWday : DayOfWeekType);

BEGIN
    Write('This will name the day using ');
    WriteLn(WDOWday)
END;    {WriteDayOfWeek}

PROCEDURE WriteDayOfYear(WDOYday : DayOfYearType);

BEGIN
    Write('Day number will be output using ');
    WriteLn(WDOYday)
END;    {WriteDayOfYear}
```

The unit dependency diagram for the original files used in this chapter is as follows:

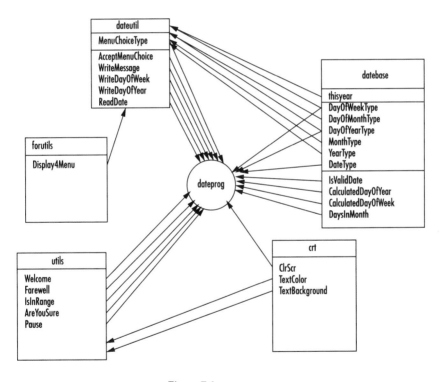

Figure 7.1

The unit dependency diagram illustrates the relationship between the various units and the main program. Whilst Exercise 7.1 specified a particular order in which the units should be compiled, there are variations which could be made to the order, provided that all units are compiled before other units which depend on them.

The procedure Display4Menu has been included in a separate file, forutils.pas, so that you can be supplied with new code to put into utils. It uses some new ideas, and its code appears as follows:

```
UNIT forutils;
{
    Utilities library
    contains any code which might be useful in later case studies
    Written by AMC/MPW
    1:1:96
}
INTERFACE

PROCEDURE Display4Menu(D4Mmessage1, D4Mmessage2, D4Mmessage3,
                       D4Mmessage4 : STRING);
{
        Pre-condition:      parameters contain the four messages to be
                            displayed as part of the menu
        Action:             displays a menu of four items, numbered 1 to
                            4, each on a separate line, with the menu
                            entries being the four messages given as
                            parameters, in the order given
        Post-condition:     none
}
IMPLEMENTATION

PROCEDURE Display4Menu(D4Mmessage1, D4Mmessage2, D4Mmessage3,
                       D4Mmessage4 : STRING);

BEGIN
    WriteLn('1. ',D4Mmessage1);
    WriteLn('2. ',D4Mmessage2);
    WriteLn('3. ',D4Mmessage3);
    WriteLn('4. ',D4Mmessage4)
END;    {Display4Menu}

END.    {forutils}
```

The procedure Display4Menu accepts four messages, all of which are held as type string. The pervasive type string is capable of holding a group of characters. A variable of this type can be assigned a value using a string literal. You have seen string literals before, particularly in WriteLn statements. The characters which form the string are represented between a pair of single quote marks (' ').

The four parameters are then output as the four elements of a menu, with each menu entry being numbered consecutively from 1 to 4. This procedure could be used by other programs to display any four-entry menu using a single instruction. The method could also be adapted to provide for menus with numbers other than four. This would entail writing extra procedures, though this could be done by copying using an editor.

The next exercise enhances the program so that it reflects the specification.

EXERCISE 7.2

Step 1. Write down an alternative order in which the units could be compiled.

Step 2. Write a new procedure, a replacement WriteMessage in dateutil, so that it displays different messages, depending on the value passed in as a parameter, as described in the specification given.

Compile the appropriate code and run the program. Using a test plan, ensure that it produces the desired output.

Step 3. Write a similar new procedure for WriteDayOfWeek. For this, you will need to use a case statement. Notice that the procedure can be written on the assumption that it is only ever passed numbers in the range 1 to 7. Ensure that the output message reflects the one included in the table of messages above. You will be able to access the year set in datebase, held as thisyear.

Compile the appropriate code and run the program. Using a test plan, ensure that it produces the desired output.

Step 4. Write WriteDayOfYear, which will output a better message than that currently provided, as specified in the table of messages above.

Compile the appropriate code and run the program. Using a test plan, ensure that it produces the desired output.

Step 5. Re-organise the libraries by including in utils the procedure provided in forutils.

7.4 Enhancing the program

If you have tested your program with any data which is not valid, you will find that, in many cases, the program does not generally 'crash', but an apparently correct answer is given for invalid data. This is because the data is not checked for validity before options 2 or 3 are chosen.

EXERCISE 7.3

Step 1. Adapt the procedure which accepts the menu choice, so that only values from 1 to 4 will be accepted, with an error message and the menu re-displayed if invalid inputs are given by the user. This will mean that the if statement in the program can be removed.

Step 2. Adapt the program dateprog so that the date is accepted. If it is invalid, a message is displayed, otherwise the day of the week and the day number are displayed.

In order to do this, you will need to remove the case statement, and use a new if statement.

Step 3. Devise and implement a test plan for the new program.

7.5 Exploring errors in programs

As you develop complex programs it is quite possible that there will be errors in your code. These are described as syntax errors and logic errors. If a syntax error is made, the program will not compile. When a program has a logic error it will compile, and will run, but it does not do what it was intended to do. The logic errors which are the most difficult to spot are those which produce sensible looking results which are incorrect. Run-time errors become apparent because the program 'crashes', and happen when a problem occurs when running the program, from which the program cannot recover, such as dividing by zero, or entering an input of the wrong type.

EXERCISE 7.4

Step 1. Try introducing the following syntax errors to one of your programs from earlier exercises in this chapter; make notes on the error messages, and the appropriate correction which is made.

(a) call a procedure with too few parameters;
(b) call a procedure with too many parameters;
(c) miss out a semi-colon (';');
(d) miss out a BEGIN;
(e) miss out an END;
(f) omit the word 'PROGRAM';
(g) miss out the final full stop ('.');
(h) call a procedure with one of the parameters of the wrong type.

Step 2. Try introducing the following logic errors to your program from Exercise 7.2; make notes on the error messages, and the appropriate correction which is made.

(a) call one procedure when you should call another;
(b) call a procedure with a parameter of the wrong name, but the right type;
(c) omit an option within a case statement.

7.6 Understanding how the units work

You have used datebase so far without looking at how it works. This, of course, reinforces the benefits, as in many previous chapters, of using clearly specified procedures and functions without analysing how they do their jobs. The next stage is to look at how the various parts of datebase work.

The interface for DaysInMonth is as follows:

```
FUNCTION DaysInMonth(DIMmonth : MonthType) : DayOfMonthType;
{
        Pre-condition:      is sent data in a MonthType as the parameter
        Action:             determines the number of days in the month
                            given
        Post-condition:     returns DayOfMonthType value containing the
                            number of days
}
```

The implementation of DaysInMonth is:

```
FUNCTION DaysInMonth(DIMmonth : MonthType) : DayOfMonthType;

VAR lDIMdays : DayOfMonthType;

BEGIN
   CASE DIMmonth OF
   1,3,5,7,8,10,12      : BEGIN
```

```
                             lDIMdays := 31
                      END;
     4,6,9,11         : BEGIN
                             lDIMdays := 30
                      END;
     2                : BEGIN
                         IF thisyear MOD 4 = 0 THEN
                         BEGIN
                             lDIMdays := 29
                         END    {of first part of IF}
                         ELSE
                         BEGIN
                             lDIMdays := 28
                         END    {IF}
                      END
                      ELSE
                      BEGIN
                         lDIMdays := 0
                      END
     END;    {CASE}
     DaysInMonth := lDIMdays
   END;   {DaysInMonth}
```

This may appear at first to be rather complicated. It consists almost entirely of a case statement. It is a function which accepts a single parameter of MonthType, which is a subrange type with values in the range 1 to 12, allowing for each of the months of the year. The lists of possible values reflect the numbers of days in each month, remembering the rhyme:

Thirty days hath September,
April, June and November,
All the rest have thirty one,
Except February alone,
Which has twenty-eight days clear,
And twenty-nine in each Leap Year.

The rule for February is that it has 28 days in most years, but has an additional day (the leap day) in a leap year. Leap years must have a year number which is divisible by 4. Some century end years, such as 1900 and 2100, are not leap years. The rule is that century end years are not leap years, except every 400 years, such as in 2000. This chapter has been designed to be limited to the years 1901 to 2099, which means that all years within the range which are divisible by 4 are leap years.

The case statement reflects the rules, which is why the case where DIMmonth is 2 contains the if statement.

The Boolean function IsValidDate takes a value of type DateType and, using the Day and Month fields, determines whether the date is valid for thisyear. Its interface is:

```
FUNCTION IsValidDate(IVDdate : DateType) : BOOLEAN;
{
     Pre-condition:     is sent data in a DateType as the parameter
     Action:            determines whether the date given is a valid
                        date
```

```
            Post-condition:    returns Boolean value containing TRUE if the
                               date is a valid one, and FALSE otherwise
}
```

The implementation of IsValidDate is:

```
FUNCTION IsValidDate(IVDdate : DateType) : BOOLEAN;

VAR lIVDvalid : BOOLEAN;

BEGIN
    IF   (IVDdate.Day <= DaysInMonth(IVDdate.Month)) AND
         (IVDdate.Month <= 12) AND (IVDdate.Day > 0) AND
         (IVDdate.Month > 0) THEN
    BEGIN
       lIVDvalid := TRUE
    END    {of first part of IF}
    ELSE
    BEGIN
       lIVDvalid := FALSE
    END;    {IF}
    IsValidDate := lIVDvalid
END;    {IsValidDate}
```

The tests which are carried out, all of which must be passed for the date to be valid, are:

- the day of the month must be less than or equal to the number of days in the month (which uses DaysInMonth)
- the month number must be less than or equal to 12
- the day of the month must be greater than zero
- the month number must be greater than zero.

7.7   The definite loop

The function CalculatedDayOfYear takes a date and returns a result which is a DayOfYearType. Again this result reflects the use of the constant set in thisyear. The interface is

```
FUNCTION CalculatedDayOfYear(CDOYdate : DateType) : DayOfYearType;
{
        Pre-condition:    is sent data in a DateType as the parameter
        Action:           determines the day of the year of the given
                          date; for valid dates this is defined as the
                          number of days up to the given day of the
                          year; for invalid dates, the value is
                          undefined
        Post-condition:   returns DayOfYearType value containing the
                          day number within the year
}
```

The implementation of CalculatedDayOfYear is:

```
FUNCTION CalculatedDayOfYear (CDOYdate : DateType) : DayOfYearType;

VAR   lCDOYcount : MonthType;
      lCDOYday   : DayOfYearType;

BEGIN
   lCDOYday := CDOYdate.Day;
   IF CDOYdate.Month > 1 THEN
   BEGIN
      FOR lCDOYcount := 1 TO CDOYdate.Month - 1 DO
      BEGIN
         lCDOYday := lCDOYday + DaysInMonth(lCDOYcount)
      END;   {FOR}
   END;   {IF}
   CalculatedDayOfYear := lCDOYday
END;   {CalculatedDayOfYear}
```

This code uses a very important programming structure, the definite loop. You are already familiar with the indefinite loop for which the while construction is used. The definite loop is one in which the number of repetitions is determined before the loop is entered. The start and end values are determined once when the loop is entered, and these are then used to determine the number of repetitions. In this case, the value of lCDOYcount is successively 1, then 2, then 3, and so on, as lCDOYcount takes each successive possible value. The last value is determined by the value of the expression CDOYdate.Month − 1.

This FOR loop adds the number of days in each of the previous months to the day number input. So, for example, it would work out the day in the year of 8th April 2001 by the following method:

running total (held in lCDOYday)		8
add days in month 1	+ 31	= 39
add days in month 2	+ 28	= 67
add days in month 3	+ 31	= 98

This is based on the year 2001, which is not a leap year. If other values were placed in thisyear, the amount added for month 2 may differ.

The formal definition of the FOR loop is as follows:

```
FOR <variable> := <startvalue> TO <endvalue> DO
BEGIN
      <series of instructions>
END;
```

The series of instructions will be carried out repeatedly with the values of variable successively taking the values from startvalue to endvalue, taking each successive possible value each time round the loop.

The exceptional case is covered, when the endvalue is less than the startvalue. In this case, the series of instructions is not executed. This may appear unlikely to happen when a program is written correctly, but it is important to bear these issues in mind when writing a program. Don't assume that two input values, for example, automatically bear a particular relationship to each other.

A second version of the FOR loop allows you to count backwards:

```
FOR <variable> := <startvalue> DOWNTO <endvalue> DO
BEGIN
     <series of instructions>
END;
```

In this case, if the startvalue is less than the endvalue, the series of instructions is not executed.

```
FUNCTION CalculatedDayOfWeek(CDOWdate : DateType) : DayOfWeekType;
{
     Pre-condition:      is sent data in a DateType as the parameter
     Action:             determines the day of the week of the given
                         date; for valid dates this is defined as 1 for
                         Sunday, 2 for Monday, ... 7 for Saturday; for
                         invalid dates, the value is undefined
     Post-condition:     returns a DayOfWeekType value containing the
                         day number within the week
}
```

The one part of datebase which has so far not been examined is CalculatedDayOfWeek. This uses modulo 7 arithmetic, and is based on the knowledge that 1st January 1901 was a Tuesday. This basis has been used so that the program is more general and can process dates in both centuries.

The calculation first works out the day number within the current year.

The number of completed leap years which have elapsed since 1901 is then worked out, and held in lCDOWleapdays, as each leap year adds an extra day which has elapsed. This is calculated by subtracting 1901 from the year and dividing by 4 with an integer result. Thus, the year 1905 will produce the result 1 as one leap year (1904) has been completed. The year 1904 produces the result 0 as no leap years have been completed.

The total is then calculated of these two figures plus the number of years since 1901 (as each one of these adds a day modulo 7, because 365 is 52 weeks and 1 day). One is then added because 1st January 1901 was a Tuesday (see later).

This calculation is then reduced modulo 7, giving a result in the range 0 to 6.

One is then added to place the results correctly in the range 1 to 7.

The first one was added to ensure that 1st January 1901 returns the result 3 for Tuesday, as in this case, the day number in the year is 1, no leap years have elapsed, and no ordinary years have elapsed. One is therefore added so that when the final one is added after the modulo 7 result is taken, a result of 3 emerges. This device for correcting this particular day will, by implication, correct all the other days.

```
FUNCTION CalculatedDayOfWeek (CDOWdate : DateType) : DayOfWeekType;

VAR lCDOWday, lCDOWleapdays: INTEGER;

BEGIN
    lCDOWday := CalculatedDayOfYear(CDOWdate);
    lCDOWleapdays := (thisyear - 1901) DIV 4;
    lCDOWday := lCDOWday + (thisyear - 1901) + lCDOWleapdays + 1;
    CalculatedDayOfWeek := (lCDOWday MOD 7) + 1
END;   {CalculatedDayOfWeek}
```

EXERCISE 7.5

Step 1. Alter the value of the constant thisyear in datebase to another year of your choosing, for which you have a suitable calendar with which to check your results.

Compile the appropriate code and run the program. Using a test plan, ensure that it produces the desired output.

Step 2. Replace the function DaysInMonth, so that it receives an extra parameter, which is the year. This will make it more general. Alter all the calls to this procedure so that they too use two parameters, otherwise compilation cannot take place. At the moment, test this only for the current year, passed as a parameter.

Compile the appropriate code and run the program. Using a test plan, ensure that it produces the desired output.

Step 3. Adapt the program and any appropriate units so that the program accepts a date consisting of day, month and year, for any year from 1901 to 2099, and outputs the day of the week on which it falls.

Compile the appropriate code and run the program. Using a test plan, ensure that it produces the desired output.

EXERCISE 7.6

For these exercises, use your completed code from Exercise 7.4.

Step 1. Write a new function in dateutil, using a for ... downto loop, which calculates for a given date how many days there are left in the current year. (It might be easier to use CalculatedDayOfYear to do this, but you would not learn as much that way!)

Write a program which uses your new function, and test it.

Step 2. Write a new procedure in dateutil which, given a day number in the month, will output the day of the week on which that day number will fall for every month of the year set in datebase. You can experiment by altering the constant thisyear in datebase. You will also need to write another procedure which accepts a day number input only.

Step 3. Enhance the program by using GetDate in the system unit dos. This allows the program to access the system date, and so the program could be made to work for the current year. This exercise will require you to think about how the year is passed as a parameter, as the constant thisyear will no longer be used.

The procedure GetDate has the specification:

```
PROCEDURE GetDate(VAR Year, Month, Day, DayOfWeek : WORD);
```

where Year is in the range 1980 .. 2099
       Month is in the range 1 .. 12
       Day is in the range 1 .. 31
and   DayOfWeek is in the range 0 .. 6 (where 0 is Sunday)

The pervasive type WORD is defined as taking values in the range 0 .. 65335, and its values can be copied into integers so long as, like in this case, the values are not out of the range for integers.

EXERCISE 7.7

These exercises are designed to help you to test yourself on the knowledge which you should have acquired in reading this chapter and doing the previous exercises.

1. Describe how you would determine the correct order of compilation if you were given a set of units and a program which may use them.
2. Explain what is meant by a subrange type.
3. Describe a typical declaration of a record type with four fields.
4. Describe how the fields of a variable of a record type are accessed.
5. Explain why, in this case study, special procedures such as WriteDayOfWeek and WriteDayOfYear have to be written in order to output values of the user-defined types. State which variable types do not need specially written procedures for output.
6. If you wished to display a menu of six items, how would you produce an adapted version of Display4Menu, called Display6Menu?
7. Why does WriteMessage have a single parameter, and why is it a value parameter?
8. Explain the difference between logic errors and syntax errors.
9. Explain the difference between a definite loop and an indefinite loop. Suggest situations in which each is more appropriate.
10. CalculatedDayOfYear is currently implemented as a function. Would it have been better if it had been implemented as a procedure?

8
The bank

Before starting this chapter, you should be able to do the following:

- use the Pascal environment to edit, compile and run
- design and use a test plan
- use a unit dependency diagram
- use selection statements
- write and use procedures and functions with parameters
- carry out arithmetic on real and integer quantities
- format output
- use definite and indefinite loops
- use subrange types
- declare and use records.

Before tackling this case study you should have produced a utilities unit containing the following:

- Welcome
- Farewell
- Pause
- RestoreColour
- AskForPin
- CheckPin
- IsInRange
- AreYouSure
- Display4Menu.

After tackling this case study you should understand:

- the 'with' notation for records
- one-dimensional arrays.

No new items are added to the utilities unit during this chapter.

8.1 Introduction

In this case study, you will be working on a simplified banking system involving automated telling machines (ATMs). Your program will keep track of the financial standing of a number of customers, each of whom can enter their name and PIN and then withdraw money from their account. At the start of a day's trading, the bank manager will initialise the system, and at the end of the day she will produce a new balance list and shut down the program.

You will be given a ready-written unit, bankbase, which contains procedures for doing some of the tasks outlined above, and will need to write your own unit, bankutil, for some of the other tasks. This time, you will also need to write the main program.

8.2   The program specification

When the program is loaded at the start of the day, a welcome message and then the bank's logo appear on the screen.

The manager presses any key to clear the screen, and then enters her special start-of-day PIN. This can be any number which is valid for CheckPin. If the number is invalid, the program terminates immediately. If the number is valid the Initialise and StartTheDay procedures are run, and a balance list is displayed on the screen.

The logo reappears, together with an invitation to customers to use the ATM. A customer enters his or her name, PIN, and the amount of money required. Note that the amount will always be a whole number of pounds. Checks are made to ensure that the PIN matches the name, that sufficient funds are available in the account, and that the daily withdrawal limit has not been exceeded. A suitable message is displayed on the screen, and the customer's details (i.e. balance and amount withdrawn today) updated if necessary. The logo then reappears, ready for the next customer.

At the end of the day, the manager enters a dummy account name, which is literally the word 'DUMMY', followed by the same PIN entered at the start of the day. A new balance list is displayed on the screen, and the program is terminated.

Note that the data is not stored permanently, so that each time the program is run it starts with the same data. This is, of course, unrealistic, but it does make the program easier to test as account balances are known, and the same at the start of every program run. Storage of data between program runs, using files, will be covered in Chapter 10.

Useful additional information

You can find out the customers' names, PINs and daily withdrawal limits by calling the procedure DisplayConfidential in the unit bankbase – but you won't want to do this in your main program! You will therefore have to write a small program just to obtain this information.

EXERCISE 8.1

Decide exactly what the program has to do, and explain the structure of the program in your own words.

Write a series of steps which show the main tasks of the program, e.g.

1. Display logo.
2. Display welcome message for manager.
3. ... etc.

8.3   The unit bankbase

You are provided with a library unit bankbase, the interface section of which is given below.

```
INTERFACE

CONST MaxCust    = 10;

TYPE NameType   =   STRING[30];
     Customer   =   RECORD
                    name : NameType;
                    accountno : INTEGER;
                    pin : INTEGER;
                    balance : REAL;
                    dailylimit : INTEGER;
                    drawntoday : INTEGER;
     END {record};
     List = ARRAY [1..MaxCust] OF Customer;

PROCEDURE Initialise (VAR Idetails : List);
{ set up details at start of program }

PROCEDURE StartTheDay (VAR STDdetails : List);
{ reset drawntoday amounts to 0, and display balance list }

PROCEDURE DisplayBalanceList (DBLdetails : List);
{ display name, accountno and balance of all customers }

PROCEDURE DisplayConfidential (DCdetails : List);
{ display name, accountno, pin, and dailylimit of all customers }

FUNCTION PinValid (PVcustname : NameType; PVcustpin : INTEGER;
                   PVdetails : List): BOOLEAN;
{ return Boolean value, depending on whether pin is valid }

PROCEDURE UpdateBalance(UBcustname : NameType;
                        UBamountdrawn : INTEGER;
                        VAR UBdetails: List);
{ update customer's record with new balance and drawntoday, when a
  withdrawal is made, but give error message if insufficient funds
  or daily limit exceeded }
```

8.4 Strings, records and arrays

Look at the declarations at the start of the interface:

```
CONST MaxCust = 10;

TYPE    NameType    = STRING[30];
        Customer    = RECORD
                      name : NameType;
                      accountno : INTEGER;
                      pin : INTEGER;
```

```
                    balance : REAL;
                    dailylimit : INTEGER;
                    drawntoday : INTEGER;
            END {record};
            List = ARRAY [1..MaxCust] OF Customer;
```

First, MaxCust is declared as a constant. A constant is an identifier whose value cannot alter during the program, unlike a variable. When a quantity is fixed for the duration of a program run, but may occasionally change between runs, then it should be declared as a constant. An example would be the rate of VAT in a program which produced invoices. The VAT rate does change occasionally, but never actually during a program run. If the whole program is written in terms of the identifier vatrate, rather than using actual numerical values, then only the constant declaration need be changed when the tax rate changes. This is likely to produce far fewer errors than if numerical values throughout the program have to be changed, when it would be only too easy to omit one change.

NameType is declared as a string type. You have met a string in previous case studies. The maximum length of the string may be declared in brackets; in the example above, it is 30 characters. If no length is specified, a maximum of 255 characters is assumed. This is known as a default value. In this case study, storage is required for names. These are most unlikely to be as long as 255 characters, and so a smaller amount of storage can be used. In this case, names are to be restricted to 30 characters in length, including spaces.

Customer is declared as a record type. Several items of data need to be stored about each customer: his or her name, account number and pin, the amount of money he or she has in the account (balance), the amount of money that may be withdrawn from the account on any one day (dailylimit) and the amount that has actually been withdrawn on the current day (drawntoday). These items of data are stored as fields in the record.

Clearly, a bank is going to have far more than one customer, and a Customer record will be required for each of them. In order to store a number of data items of the same type, Pascal uses the array data structure. If the bank had only five customers, it might be appropriate to declare a type:

```
    ShortList = ARRAY [1..5] OF Customer;
```

This would allow storage for the details of up to five separate customers, indexed (or listed) from 1 to 5. Each of the five items in the list would be a record, of type customer.

If the bank had 300 customers, then the type declaration:

```
    LongList = ARRAY [1..300] OF Customer;
```

would allow storage for the details of up to 300 customers, indexed from 1 to 300.

You should recognise the numbers in brackets as being a subrange. In this case the subrange is integer, but it could be char, and need not start at 1.

For example, the variable declaration:

```
    VAR lettercount : ARRAY ['A'..'Z'] OF INTEGER;
```

would be useful if you wanted to count the number of times each letter of the alphabet occurred in a passage of text. It declares storage for 26 integers, indexed from A to Z.

So, for example, the number of letter 'E's in the passage would be stored in

```
lettercount['E']
```

and the number of letter 'T's would be given by

```
lettercount['T']
```

The variable declaration

```
rainfall : ARRAY [1985..1999] OF REAL;
```

could be used if you were recording the rainfall per year between 1985 and 1999. While

```
rainfall : ARRAY [1..15] OF REAL ;
```

could also be used, it would be more obvious from the first declaration to which year you were referring. The declaration reserves contiguous (that is, following on) storage space for the fifteen real numbers that make up the rainfall list. You can think of it like a list or a table:

Year	Rainfall
1985	192.5
1986	160.8
1987	203.5

....

1997	221.3
1998	193.0
1999	215.7

The rainfall for an individual year can be accessed by giving the year in brackets. The year is called the array index. For example

```
rainfall[1997]
```

has the value 221.3 in the table above. The individual values in this array are real numbers, and so can be input, output, have values assigned to them, and be used in calculations, as the following examples show:

```
ReadLn(rainfall[1992]);
WriteLn('The rainfall for 1993 was ', rainfall[1993]);
rainfall[1988] := 184.9;
total85to6 := rainfall[1985] + rainfall[1986];
```

The ReadLn and WriteLn procedures only take parameters of type real, integer, char or string. Therefore, keyboard input and screen display can only be performed for individual components (which must themselves be one of these types) of an array.

The formal definition for the array type declaration is:

<type-name> = ARRAY [<lower-bound> .. <upper-bound>] OF <array-base-type>;

Clearly <lower-bound> needs to be smaller than <upper-bound>, but neither of them need be a literal value. Identifiers for constants, or even arithmetic expressions can be used. In this case study, the upper bound for List is declared in terms of the constant identifier MaxCust. At present, MaxCust has the value 10. But if the bank later expands to 20 or 50 or even more customers, the only alteration needed will be to the constant declaration at the start.

In order to use a variable of type List in the main program, you will have to declare it in the normal way. For example,

```
VAR customerlist: List;
```

customerlist can then be used in a number of ways. Firstly, customerlist refers to the entire list. As such, it can be copied to another list declared to be of the same type, using a simple assignment statement:

```
VAR clist1, clist2 : List;
. . .
. . .
clist1 := clist2;
```

In this case, the components of the array are on two levels. First, the array is made up of a number of records, and then each record is composed of a number of fields. The subrange used to declare the bounds of the array is also used to access the individual records, and within each record the individual fields are accessed using their field names, as seen in the last chapter.

Given the declarations:

```
TYPE ShortList = ARRAY [1..5] OF Customer;
VAR custlist : ShortList;
```

then it is clear that storage space has been reserved for the records of five customers. The subrange 1..5 is used to index the five records comprising the array, and so the individual records may be accessed as:

```
custlist[1]
custlist[2]
custlist[3]
custlist[4]
custlist[5]
```

and individual fields may be accessed by combining the fieldname with the record identifier. So:

```
custlist[1].name
```

will be the identifier for the name of the first customer in the list;

```
custlist[5].balance
```

will be the identifier for the bank balance of the fifth customer in the list, and so on.

Entire records may be copied with assignment statements, for example:

```
custlist[3] := custlist[2];
```

will copy the contents of the second record into the third.

However, individual fields may be manipulated in the same way as simple variables of the same type. So, balances may have arithmetic performed on them, as may the drawntoday field. The following statement will amend the balance of customer 5 by subtracting amountdrawn from it:

```
custlist[5].balance := custlist[5].balance - amountdrawn;
```

To display on the screen all the data for one particular customer you would need to display each field separately:

```
WriteLn(custlist[4].name, custlist[4].accountno, custlist[4].pin,
        custlist[4].balance:7:2, custlist[4].dailylimit,
        custlist[4].drawntoday);
```

As an alternative, Pascal allows the 'with' notation or statement to refer to a particular record:

```
WITH custlist[4] DO
BEGIN
      WriteLn(name, accountno, pin, balance:7:2, dailylimit,
              drawntoday)
END;
```

Fieldnames such as name, accountno, etc. within the WriteLn statement are said to be 'unqualified' as the record name is not specified. Any unqualified fieldname inside the scope of the with statement (i.e. between the begin and end) is taken to belong to the record specified by with. So the two code fragments above perform the same task.

Notice that only balance contains formatting. The default output formats can be used for the other quantities, although formatting would produce neater output. However, balance is a currency amount which might involve pence as well as pounds and therefore really should be formatted with two decimal places. The output could be further improved by adding captions, and £ signs to the currency amounts. This would be done using literals in the WriteLn parameter list:

```
WITH custlist[4] DO
BEGIN
    WriteLn('Name: ', name, 'Account: ', accountno:4, 'Pin: ', pin:4,
            'Balance £', balance:7:2, 'Dailylimit £', dailylimit:1,
            'Drawn today £', drawntoday:1)
END;
```

Look at the procedure Initialise in the implementation section of bankbase. This is the procedure which sets up all the bank accounts by assigning values to the various fields. It is a long procedure, as it is a long and tedious task. However, as every account is different, each field must be assigned individually. Use is made of the with statement for each record in turn, to reduce the amount of repetitive typing. The following statements could be used to set up the account for the first customer:

```
Idetails[1].name := 'Elizabeth Brown';
Idetails[1].accountno := 2363;
Idetails[1].pin := 3632;
Idetails[1].balance := 47.66;
Idetails[1].dailylimit := 10;
```

The with statement allows the array and index to be omitted, resulting in a section of code which is easier to read:

```
WITH Idetails[1] DO
BEGIN
    name := 'Elizabeth Brown';
    accountno := 2363;
    pin := 3632;
    balance := 47.66;
    dailylimit := 10;
END {WITH 1};
```

The set of assignment statements needs to be repeated for each customer in turn:

```
WITH Idetails[2] DO
BEGIN
    name := 'George Red';
    accountno := 1237;
    pin := 3572;
    balance := 2.01;
    dailylimit := 1;
END {WITH 2};
WITH Idetails[3] DO
BEGIN
    name := 'Edward Orange';
    accountno := 9999;
    pin := 1111;
    balance := 467.12;
    dailylimit := 50;
END {WITH 3};
WITH Idetails[4] DO
BEGIN
    name := 'Victoria Yellow';
    accountno := 4362;
    pin := 5432;
    balance := 129.39;
    dailylimit := 20;
```

```
END {WITH 4};
WITH Idetails[5] DO
BEGIN
   name := 'William Green';
   accountno := 1357;
   pin := 2468;
   balance := 93.47;
   dailylimit := 20;
END {WITH 5};
WITH Idetails[6] DO
BEGIN
   name := 'Anne Blue';
   accountno := 7219;
   pin := 9120;
   balance := 81.73;
   dailylimit := 20;
END {WITH 6};
WITH Idetails[7] DO
BEGIN
   name := 'Mary Violet';
   accountno := 8042;
   pin := 7531;
   balance := 9999.99;
   dailylimit := 300;
END {WITH 7};
WITH Idetails[8] DO
BEGIN
   name := 'James Grey';
   accountno := 3115;
   pin := 4967;
   balance := 305.84;
   dailylimit := 50;
END {WITH 8};
WITH Idetails[9] DO
BEGIN
   name := 'Charles White';
   accountno := 9649;
   pin := 9496;
   balance := 53.49;
   dailylimit := 15;
END {WITH 9};
WITH Idetails[10] DO
BEGIN
   name := 'Henry Black';
   accountno := 1061;
   pin := 6187;
   balance := 61.20;
   dailylimit := 15;
END {WITH 10};
```

EXERCISE 8.2

Write pre- and post-conditions and action descriptions for each of the procedures in bankbase.

Add them to the file, and ensure that it will still compile.

(Hint: if the unit will not compile, and the error messages are not obvious, check that all the comment braces are properly paired.)

8.5   Time management

Clearly you cannot write the whole program all at once. You will have to decide on an order for doing it.

EXERCISE 8.3

The list below gives some of the tasks you will need to do when you write the program. Put the list in order, labelling each task for completion in Stage 1 ... Stage 5. Some tasks may need doing a number of times, and others have been omitted and need to be added to the list. In the final column you can give your reasons for your choice of order.

Task	Stage	Reason
1. Compile bankbase		
2. Test program		
3. Write algorithm for main program		
4. Write end-of-day algorithm		
5. Compile main program		
6. Code logo		
7. Write start-of-day algorithm		
8. Design logo		
9. Compile bankutil		
10. Dry run main program		
11. Code screen dialogue for customer withdrawals		
12.		
13.		
14.		
15.		
16.		

8.6   The main program

You will need to create another unit, bankutil, to contain the procedures you write for this case study. You are also going to need to write some programs which use the library units.

A suggested interface section of bankutil is given below, and is available on disk as chap8\bankutil.pas. The procedures and functions are currently all dummies, that is, their correct code in the implementation section has not yet been written. You will also need to add extra procedures, e.g. for the customer to enter his or her details before withdrawing any money. Note that dummy procedures contain even less than the skeleton procedures you have used previously. A dummy procedure does nothing at all, but does at least allow the main program to be compiled. A dummy function must return a result, although it will contain an arbritrary result to return, and not calculate the correct result.

```
FUNCTION SamePins(SPoldmasterpin, SPnewmasterpin: INTEGER) :
                  BOOLEAN;
{  compare two pin numbers to see whether they are the same }

PROCEDURE DrawLogo;
{ draw logo on screen }

PROCEDURE WelcomeCust;
{  used between customers,  to display welcome message to customer
   wishing to use ATM }
```

EXERCISE 8.4

Write pre- and post-conditions and action descriptions for each of the procedures in bankutil.

EXERCISE 8.5

Use the algorithm that you wrote in Exercise 8.1 to write the main program, which uses the (yet to be written) procedures of bankutil, the provided library unit bankbase, and utils. Test that it compiles with the dummy procedures and functions in bankutil, and runs, and that you have passed parameters correctly.

8.7   Dry running a program

You will not be able to test the program with any data at this stage, because the procedures in bankutil which input and process data have not yet been written in detail. However, a dry run of the program is possible at this stage. It is important to check that procedures and functions are called in the correct order and with the right data passed to them and information returned. A dry run is a pencil and paper exercise, and involves tracing the changes made to a set of data as it passes through the program. It can be a tedious exercise, and is often better performed by someone other than the original programmer, as he or she will be more likely to follow the actual path taken and calculations performed, rather than the intended path and calculations. It is possible to think that you know a program so well that you misread what you actually programmed for what you intended to program; an outsider taking a fresh look at the code is more likely to spot this.

You will probably find it helpful to use a 'trace table' for your dry run. This is a table in which you list the changes made to the relevant variables at each stage of the program.

EXERCISE 8.6

Dry run your overall program structure with a suitable set of test data.

8.8   Making withdrawals

You now need to write the part of the program which allows customers to withdraw money. You can leave the start-of-day routine as dummy procedures which will be coded later, as this part of the program does not generate any data needed by the main processing section of the program. However, you must call Initialise (in bankbase) to set up the account information at the start of the program, otherwise none of the other procedures and functions can be tested.

You will need procedures in your library for entering and checking a customer's details, and then updating the master list if the details are valid. These procedures will in turn call the appropriate procedures in bankbase. You should use the account name 'DUMMY' to exit the loop and terminate the program. You will code this part later.

EXERCISE 8.7

Step 1. Before you can test the program, you will need to know who the customers are, and what their PINs and withdrawal limits are. You could find out the information by reading through the code in bankbase, but a better solution to the problem is to write a different short program which makes use of the procedure DisplayConfidential, as mentioned in Section 8.2. Call this program 'bankconf'.

Step 2. Write the procedures needed for making withdrawals and test the program.

8.9   Completing the program

Now that the main processing part of the program has been written, the set-up and termination procedures need to be completed.

EXERCISE 8.8

Step 1. Design a suitable logo for the bank's ATM. Remember that a simple design can be very effective. Code it as a procedure which will go in bankutil, and write a simple program to test it alone.

Step 2. Write the procedures, and any amendments needed to the main program, to perform the set-up stages before the first customer uses the ATM.
   Record any testing that you do.

Step 3. Now complete the program by adding the code to terminate the program according to the specification given.
   Do not forget to record carefully your testing.

Step 4. Look back at the plan you made in Exercise 8.3, and compare it with the order of solution and coding suggested in this book. Which order do you think is better? Why?

EXERCISE 8.9

These exercises are designed to help you to test yourself on the knowledge which you should have acquired in reading this chapter and doing the previous exercises.

1. What is the advantage of limiting the length of a variable of type string?
2. What is an array?
3. What is meant by the index of an array?
4. Explain what is meant by array bound. Devise examples which set the array bounds using
   (a) literals;
   (b) constants.
5. Explain the statement that 'custlist is an array of records, each with several fields'. Can you have an array as a field of a record?
6. Explain the two possible notations to access fields of a record.
7. Why was it most sensible to code the bank's logo towards the end of your tasks?
8. Explain whether you believe it would have been better to code the screen dialogue early or late in the development process.
9. Why is the function SamePins a Boolean function? Could the test have been better done without a function?
10. Is the order in which the ten records are set in Initialise significant?

9
Further dates

Before tackling this chapter it is essential that you are able to do the following:

- use the Pascal environment to edit, compile and run
- design and use a test plan
- use a unit dependency diagram
- use selection statements
- write and use procedures and functions with parameters
- carry out arithmetic on real and integer quantities
- format output
- use definite and indefinite loops
- use subrange types
- declare and use records
- use one-dimensional arrays.

Before tackling this chapter you will have produced a utilities unit, completed in Chapter 7.

After tackling this chapter you should understand:

- the basis of organising code into different units
- the use of arrays of more than one dimension
- the use of enumerated types.

No new items are added to the utilities unit during this chapter.

9.1   Organising the units

In the previous chapters, there has been a particular pattern to the organisation of units. Many of the previous chapters have used four units. One of these is crt, which is a system unit, over which the programmer has no control. The typical organisation of units reflected in the code which you have already seen, and described on unit dependency diagrams, has been to write a main program that uses three units apart from crt. The file utils.pas has been one that has built up from chapter to chapter. This has been used to collect together code which may be useful to any of the case studies in the future, so procedures like Welcome, Farewell and Pause are used in a wide range of cases.

Most of the cases studied so far have also used two other units specific to the cases. The first has had a name ending with 'base', and has usually contained the pre-written code for the chapter. Each chapter has described what is contained in the interface section of such files. The second, case-specific, file has usually had a name ending in 'util'. Initially, this perhaps contained code which you were expected simply to read and understand, but later you were asked to alter code provided in such units, perhaps with a skeleton or dummy version provided for you, so that the collection of files provided with the chapter would immediately compile, even if it did not carry out the full specification.

Before you commence this new chapter, which takes the manipulation of dates further, though, there is an opportunity to redefine this boundary between the 'base' and 'util' file for a case study. In more recent chapters, you have been required to look at and alter the code in both of these files, so the initial distinction which was drawn between 'files to alter' and 'files not to alter' has been removed. From now on, the two files should be distinguished by putting code in the 'base' file if it is likely to be used for other programs on the same theme, but to include it in the 'util' file if it is being written specifically for a particular program to use.

This would mean, in the date case study of Chapter 7, for example, that procedures such as WriteDay, which was previously placed in dateutil, would be better placed in datebase. Based on this new division between the two files, in the new case study 'diary', the various declarations should be allocated between 'diarbase' and 'diarutil' according to the following table:

Declaration	Chapter 7	Chapter 9
DayOfWeekType	datebase	diarbase
DayOfMonthType	datebase	diarbase
DayOfYearType	datebase	diarbase
MonthType	datebase	diarbase
YearType	datebase	diarbase
DateType	datebase	diarbase
DaysInMonth	datebase	diarbase
CalculatedDayOfWeek	datebase	diarbase
CalculatedDayNumber	datebase	diarbase
IsValidDate	datebase	diarbase
ReadDay	dateutil	diarbase
ReadMonth	dateutil	diarbase
ReadYear	dateutil	diarbase
ReadDate	dateutil	diarbase
WriteDay	dateutil	diarbase
WriteMonth	dateutil	diarbase
WriteYear	dateutil	diarbase
WriteDate	dateutil	diarbase
WriteFullDate	dateutil	diarbase
WriteDayNo	dateutil	diarbase
MenuChoice	dateutil	diarutil
AcceptMenuChoice	dateutil	diarutil
WriteMessage	dateutil	diarutil

EXERCISE 9.1

Re-organise the files from Chapter 7 to produce the two new units diarbase and diarutil.

9.2   Manipulating an array of dates

The problems in Chapter 7 involved the manipulation of one date at a time. This chapter looks at some problems which illustrate the use of a popular problem solving technique in computing, which is the production of a solution by elimination, or a 'sieve' method.

Elimination methods are based on the idea of generating every possible solution for a problem, and then checking whether each solution fits the rules. These methods are very suitable for some problem solving by computer.

Take, for example, the problem of displaying all the Sundays in September 2002. The method is as follows:

1. Produce a list of all possible dates in September 2002 (there are 30 of them).
2. Work out the day of the week for every date in the list.
3. Display those dates in the list which are Sundays.

The advantage of this method for a computer solution is that each of these steps is relatively simple. The disadvantage of such a method for operation by humans is that it is long-winded and error-prone. These two disadvantages do not apply to a computer program, as computers are both quick and accurate.

The suggested main program for the solution appears as follows:

```
PROGRAM diary;
{
     Main program for Chapter 9 - More dates
     Displays all the dates which fall on a given day in a given
     month
     Written by AMC/MPW
     1:1:96

}
USES diarutil, diarbase, utils, crt;

VAR  inday      : DayOfWeekType;
     inmonth    : MonthType;
     inyear     : YearType;
     possdates  : DateArrayType;

BEGIN
     Welcome;
     Explain;
     ReadDayOfWeek(inday);
     ReadMonth(inmonth);
     ReadYear(inyear);
     GenerateTable(inmonth, inyear, possdates);
```

```
    GenerateDays(possdates);
    OutputHeadings(inday, inmonth, inyear);
    WriteChosenDays(possdates, inday);
    Pause;
    Farewell;
    RestoreColour
END.  {diary}
```

The core of this solution lies in the three procedures GenerateTable, GenerateDays and WriteChosenDays.

The specifications of these procedures, which should appear in diarutil, are as follows:

```
PROCEDURE GenerateTable(GTmonth : MonthType;
         GTyear : YearType; VAR GTdates : DateArrayType);
{
     Pre-condition:     is sent data in a MonthType as the first
                        parameter, and a YearType as the second
                        parameter; the third parameter is ignored
     Action:            generates an array of dates containing every
                        day in the given month and the given year
     Post-condition:    returns the array in data structure of type
                        DateArrayType

}
PROCEDURE GenerateDays(VAR GDdates : DateArrayType);
{
     Pre-condition:     is sent data in a DateArrayType as the
                        parameter
     Action:            determines the days of week of each entry in
                        the array of dates and sets the value of the
                        DayOfWeek field to the day which is determined
     Post-condition:    returns the array in data structure of type
                        DateArrayType

}
PROCEDURE WriteChosenDays(WCDdates : DateArrayType;
         WCDdaychosen : DayOfWeekType);
{
     Pre-condition:     is sent data in a DateArrayType, representing
                        all the dates in a particular month, as the
                        first parameter, and a DayOfWeekType as the
                        second parameter
     Action:            displays the day of the month of every entry
                        in the DateArrayType where the day matches
                        the second parameter
     Post-condition:    none
}
```

The data table to be manipulated by these three procedures has the following declaration.

```
TYPE DateArrayType = ARRAY[1..31] OF DateType;
```

The type is declared in diarutil, because it is specific to the particular problem, rather than being generally applicable to several problems of this sort.

The actions of the three procedures together will first fill the array with the days in the selected month, completing the day, month and year fields, then pass through the list a second time inserting the day of the week, and then finally will output only the days where the day of the week matches.

Expressing this as a list of instructions, the method will work as follows:

1. Generate a table of all the dates of the given number in the given month (an array of up to 31 dates).
2. Work through the array calculating and inserting the day of the week.
3. Work through the array outputting those dates which fall on the required day of the week.

The program requires the use of ReadDayOfWeek which, according to the rules described earlier, should be included in diarbase. At this stage, this will accept input as a number representing the day of the week. Later in the chapter, a new program will be produced allowing the input as text.

The other procedures to be included in diarutil are OutputHeadings and Explain. The former will output a message in the form 'Sundays in September 2002', and the latter will describe the purpose of the program to the user. You are asked to write the pre- and post-conditions for these procedures.

EXERCISE 9.2

Step 1. Draw the unit dependency diagram for the solution described.

Step 2. Add the procedure ReadDayOfWeek to diarbase, checking that it is correct.

Step 3. Add the procedures GenerateTable, GenerateDays, WriteChosenDays, OutputHeadings and Explain to diarutil, checking that they are correct.

Step 4. Complete the program diary from the specification and description given. Test the program thoroughly. A sample solution is provided as diary.exe on disk.

A further problem requires a similar form of solution. The requirement is for a program which accepts a day of the week (a number in the range 1 to 7), a day of the month and a year, and outputs a list of all the days of that type within the year. This program could be used, for example, to output all the Friday 13ths in 2001.

The method will work as follows:

1. Generate a table of all the dates of the given number in the given year (an array of 12 dates).
2. Work through the array calculating and inserting the day of the week.
3. Work through the array outputting those dates which fall on the required day of the week.

EXERCISE 9.3

Step 1. Draw the unit dependency diagram for the program required.

Step 2. Write the pre- and post-conditions and actions of the new procedures which you will need.

Step 3. Complete the program from the specification and description given above. Test the program thoroughly.

EXERCISE 9.4

Design, write and test a program which accepts a person's date of birth, and outputs the day on which the person's birthday will fall for the first fifty years of life.

9.3 Enumerated types

The data manipulated by the units and programs which you have seen so far to process date information has been entirely numerical. In order to limit the range of possible values, you have used subrange types, so for example, the definition of DayOfWeekType in diarbase is:

```
TYPE DayOfWeekType = 1..7;
```

and for MonthType it is:

```
MonthType = 1..12;
```

These definitions are then reflected in later definitions such as the record declaration

```
DateType = RECORD
            DayofWeek : DayOfWeekType;
            Day       : DayOfMonthType;
            Month     : MonthType;
            Year      : YearType
END   {RECORD};
```

and in procedures and functions which use these types, such as:

```
PROCEDURE WriteDayOfWeek(WDOWday : DayOfWeekType);
```

Though the use of numbers for days of the week and months of the year appears perfectly natural, there are occasions when it is more difficult to apply a numeric value to a variable, such as the storage of a colour – there is no natural way of giving colours numbers. Pascal allows you to define a variable type by saying exactly what values it can take. As all the values have to be listed, or enumerated, this variable type is called an 'enumerated type'.

There are a number of rules to the declaration of an enumerated type. The identifiers used as the values in the list must not be used elsewhere in the unit or program as identifiers. No values used by one enumerated type can be used by another enumerated type. This can lead to a limitation which is overcome later.

A typical enumerated type declaration, for DayOfWeek type, to replace the subrange type used before, looks like this:

```
TYPE DayOfWeekType = (Sunday, Monday, Tuesday, Wednesday, Thursday,
                      Friday, Saturday);
```

This defines all possible values that any variable or parameter of type DayOfWeekType may take. Notice that the values in the list enclosed in brackets are not surrounded by inverted commas. They are not strings; they are identifiers, and must follow the rules for identifiers. They are declared in a particular order, and that will be important in their later use.

Similarly, the definition of MonthType as an enumerated type could be:

```
MonthType = (January, February, March, April, May, June, July,
            August, September, October, November, December);
```

The next exercises will involve the conversion of the 'diar' suite (namely diarbase, diarutil and diary) into a version which will carry out the same tasks, but using enumerated types.

It is important to notice that this will not involve any substantial changes to the util unit or the main program. This is because changes are only being made to the underlying storage of data, not to the procedures which use that data.

The interface section of diarutil is:

```
INTERFACE

USES crt, diarbase;

TYPE DateArrayType = ARRAY[1..31] OF DateType;

PROCEDURE GenerateTable(GTmonth : MonthType;
                        GTyear  : YearType; VAR GTdates :
                        DateArrayType);
{
        Pre-condition:      is sent data in a MonthType as the first
                            parameter, and a YearType as the second
                            parameter; the third parameter is ignored
        Action:             generates an array of dates containing every
                            day in the given month and the given year
        Post-condition:     returns the array in data structure of type
                            DateArrayType
}
PROCEDURE GenerateDays(VAR GDdates : DateArrayType);
{
        Pre-condition:      is sent data in a DateArrayType as the
                            parameter
        Action:             determines the days of week of each entry in
                            the array of dates and sets the value of the
                            DayOfWeek field to the day which is
                            determined
        Post-condition:     returns the array in data structure of type
                            DateArrayType
}
PROCEDURE OutputHeadings(OHday : DayOfWeekType; OHmonth :
                         MonthType; OHyear : YearType);
{
        Pre-condition:      is sent data in a DayOfWeekType as the first
                            parameter, data in a MonthType as the second
```

```
                          parameter, and data in a YearType as the
                          third parameter
       Action:            displays the day name, followed by 's in ',
                          then the month name and the year;  for
                          example 'Mondays in September 2002'
       Post-condition:    none
 }
 PROCEDURE WriteChosenDays(WCDdates : DateArrayType;
                          WCDdaychosen : DayOfWeekType);
 {
       Pre-condition:     is sent data in a DateArrayType,
                          representing all the dates in a particular
                          month, as the first parameter, and a
                          DayOfWeekType as the second parameter
       Action:            displays the day of the month of every entry
                          in the DateArrayType where the day matches
                          the second parameter
       Post-condition:    none
 }
 PROCEDURE Explain;
 {
       Pre-condition:     none
       Action:            displays message explaining the function of
                          the program
       Post-condition:    none
 }
```

The definitions of DayOfWeekType and MonthType will have to be altered in the 'base' file, along with all procedures and functions which manipulate them.

Those to be altered are:

```
PROCEDURE   WriteDayOfWeek(WDOWday : DayOfWeekType);
PROCEDURE   WriteMonth(WMmonth : MonthType);
FUNCTION    DaysInMonth(DIMmonth : MonthType; DIMyear: YearType)
            : DayOfMonthType;
FUNCTION    CalculatedDayOfYear(CDOYdate : DateType) : DayOfYearType;
FUNCTION    CalculatedDayOfWeek(CDOWdate : DateType) : DayOfWeekType;
FUNCTION    IsValidDate(IVDdate : DateType) : BOOLEAN;
PROCEDURE   WriteFullDate(WFDdate : DateType);
PROCEDURE   ReadDayOfWeek(VAR RDOWday : DayOfWeekType);
PROCEDURE   ReadMonth(VAR RMmonth : MonthType);
```

Notice that a procedure such as ReadDate need not be altered as it is only affected indirectly. It calls procedures which need to be changed, but need not be changed itself.

```
 PROCEDURE ReadDate(VAR RDdate : DateType);

 BEGIN
      ReadDayOfMonth(RDdate.Day);
      ReadMonth(RDdate.Month);
      ReadYear(RDdate.Year)
 END;
```

WriteFullDate is in the same category.

A variable of type DayOfWeekType can be assigned a value from the list of possible values in the declaration. This is illustrated by the new version of Calculated DayOfWeek:

```
FUNCTION CalculatedDayOfWeek(CDOWdate : DateType) : DayOfWeekType;

VAR lCDOWday, lCDOWleapdays: INTEGER;

BEGIN
   lCDOWday := CalculatedDayOfYear(CDOWdate);
   lCDOWleapdays := (CDOWdate.Year - 1901) DIV 4;
   lCDOWday := lCDOWday + (CDOWdate.Year - 1901)
              + lCDOWleapdays + 1;
   lCDOWday := (lCDOWday MOD 7) + 1;
   CASE lCDOWday OF
   1 : BEGIN CalculatedDayOfWeek := Sunday END;
   2 : BEGIN CalculatedDayOfWeek := Monday END;
   3 : BEGIN CalculatedDayOfWeek := Tuesday END;
   4 : BEGIN CalculatedDayOfWeek := Wednesday END;
   5 : BEGIN CalculatedDayOfWeek := Thursday END;
   6 : BEGIN CalculatedDayOfWeek := Friday END;
   7 : BEGIN CalculatedDayOfWeek := Saturday END;
   END;   {of CASE}
END;   {CalculatedDayOfWeek}
```

Here the calculation is exactly the same as in the previous version, but the value is given to CalculatedDayOfWeek, declared as a function of type DayOfWeekType. The values on the right-hand side of the seven assignment statements are of type DayOfWeekType. Note that the allocation of the values within the case statement could be done in any order, and do not depend on the order in which values are declared in the type declaration. Note also that to save space the single command is shown on the same line as begin and end which relate to it.

The function DaysInMonth uses the possible values of DIMmonth as elements within a case statement. This version makes the code more readable than the numerically based version, and coding in this form is less prone to errors, and errors are made easier to spot.

```
FUNCTION DaysInMonth(DIMmonth : MonthType; DIMyear: YearType)
         : DayOfMonthType;

VAR lDIMdaysinmonth : DayOfMonthType;

BEGIN
   CASE DIMmonth OF
   January, March, May,
   July, August, October,
   December                       : BEGIN
                                        lDIMdaysinmonth := 31
                                    END;   {branch of CASE}
   April, June, September,
   November                       : BEGIN
                                        lDIMdaysinmonth := 30
                                    END;   {branch of CASE}
```

```
February              : BEGIN
                          IF DIMyear MOD 4 = 0 THEN
                          BEGIN
                              1DIMdaysinmonth := 29
                          END   {of first part of IF}
                          ELSE
                          BEGIN
                              1DIMdaysinmonth := 28
                          END   {IF}
                        END   {branch of CASE}
    END;    {CASE}
    DaysInMonth := 1DIMdaysinmonth;
  END;    {DaysInMonth}
```

One initial frustration in the use of enumerated types is that they cannot be used with ReadLn and WriteLn (nor with Read and Write). This means that special Read and Write routines have to be written for each enumerated type you declare and which needs input and output, but this is not as big an imposition as it sounds, as these can be written fairly quickly to a standard format. In this exercise, the existing form of input is retained, but the output procedures are replaced. The refinement of the input procedures will be tackled later in the chapter.

It is worth remarking that the pervasive procedures Read and Write, and their 'Ln' counterparts, are quite remarkable in nature. They can be used with any number of parameters, of any pervasive types or subrange types of pervasive types. The definition of these procedures, therefore, is not one similar to those used in the interfaces of units described previously. Those programmers who advocate the 'object-oriented approach' might say that every type which is declared should have its own distinct input and output procedures. The limitation that Pascal's input and output procedures cannot be used with enumerated types simply forces this upon you.

The typical output procedure, here specially written to output a DayOfWeekType, consists of a case statement identifying every possible value of a parameter of this type, with the output of a string for each one. It is therefore of a very similar style to the previous version where the day of the week was held internally as a numeric value and was converted on output. It is coded as follows:

```
PROCEDURE WriteDayOfWeek(WDOWday : DayOfWeekType);

BEGIN
    CASE WDOWday OF
        Sunday :        BEGIN Write('Sunday') END;
        Monday :        BEGIN Write('Monday') END;
        Tuesday :       BEGIN Write('Tuesday') END;
        Wednesday :     BEGIN Write('Wednesday') END;
        Thursday :      BEGIN Write('Thursday') END;
        Friday :        BEGIN Write('Friday') END;
        Saturday :      BEGIN Write('Saturday') END
    END   {of CASE}
END;    {WriteDayOfWeek}
```

This code is very simple in format, converting the 'internal' code of the enumerated type into a 'human-readable' string format.

The code for WriteMonth looks very similar. In future chapters, the code for such output will not be spelled out. By analogy, you should be able to write such code for yourself.

```
PROCEDURE WriteMonth(WMmonth : MonthType);

BEGIN
    CASE WMmonth OF
        January  :       BEGIN Write('January') END;
        February :       BEGIN Write('February') END;
        March  :         BEGIN Write('March') END;
        April  :         BEGIN Write('April') END;
        May  :           BEGIN Write('May') END;
        June  :          BEGIN Write('June') END;
        July  :          BEGIN Write('July') END;
        August  :        BEGIN Write('August') END;
        September  :     BEGIN Write('September') END;
        October  :       BEGIN Write('October') END;
        November  :      BEGIN Write('November') END;
        December  :      BEGIN Write('December') END
    END    {CASE}
END;    {WriteMonth}
```

Another function which uses MonthType will need to be altered, and that is CalculatedDayOfYear. In the numerical version described earlier, a loop is used to add to the day of the current month the total days in all the preceding months.

The replacement code uses four important properties of an enumerated type:

(a) An enumerated type can be used as the control variable of a for loop, with successive values being taken each time round the loop. These values are taken in the order in which they are declared in the type declaration. The order of the identifiers in the type declaration is therefore significant, though features which exploit the ordering of the values need not necessarily be used.

(b) An enumerated type can be used with a relational operator (such as > in the example here). Relational operators also depend on the ordering of the identifiers in the type declaration, so that 'greater than' (>) means 'comes after in the list', 'less than' means 'comes before in the list', with other operators, such as 'greater than or equals' being interpreted accordingly.

(c) An enumerated type cannot have ordinary arithmetic operations carried out on it. A function is provided so that you can access the next value in the enumerated type list. The function succ( ) requires a parameter of an enumerated type, and returns the value next in the declaration list, or causes a run-time error if the current value is the last. The function pred( ) returns the value previous in the list to the current value, with a run-time error if the current value is the first. 'Succ' is an abbreviation of successor, and 'pred' of predecessor. The run-time errors generated if the values are taken out of the defined range are generated by the system's in-built range checking. This may be turned off by the user, but then if values do go out of range, there is no guarantee what values are actually taken.

(d) The position of an enumerated type value can be determined using the ord function. This returns, as an integer, the position of the value within the declaration list, with the numbering starting at zero. 'Ord' is an abbreviation of ordinal.

In this particular example, 'ord' is not used, but it will play an important part later in this chapter.

In the previous, numerical version, the day totals for each preceding month up to but not including the current month have to be added. The numerical version required the subtraction of 1 from the month number. With an enumerated type, this is done using the 'pred' function.

The code of CalculatedDayOfYear is:

```
FUNCTION CalculatedDayOfYear(CDOYdate : DateType) : DayOfYearType;

VAR   lCDOYcount : MonthType;
      lCDOYday   : DayOfYearType;

BEGIN
   lCDOYday := CDOYdate.Day;
   IF CDOYdate.Month > January THEN
   BEGIN
      FOR lCDOYcount := January TO Pred(CDOYdate.Month) DO
      BEGIN
         lCDOYday := lCDOYday +
                   DaysInMonth(lCDOYcount, CDOYdate.Year)
      END;    {FOR}
   END;    {IF}
   CalculatedDayOfYear := lCDOYday
END;    {CalculatedDayOfYear}
```

The code for the function IsValidDate will also have to be replaced, but is not given here, as it is based on the principles explained so far.

EXERCISE 9.5

Step 1. Complete a new program suite, called 'log', 'logbase' and so on, which carries out the same actions as the program in Exercise 9.2, but uses a 'base' unit using enumerated types for days of the week and months of the year as just described.

Step 2. Produce an alternative solution, which first calculates the first and last dates in a given month (using DaysInMonth), then calls a procedure which accepts as its two parameters the first and last dates of the month (as DateType). These dates should then be written line by line using a definite loop which counts through all the day numbers. It need not calculate the day of the week for every interim day, as once the day of the week of the first of the month is known, then the days can be stepped through using the succ function. You will need to avoid the day name going out of range by detecting when the day has reached Saturday and setting the subsequent value to Sunday.

9.4   Input arrangement for enumerated types

So far, the output procedures have been changed to reflect the enumerated type now being used, but the 'log' suite still relies on numerical input for the day of the week and the month. The day of week input particularly depends on describing to the user the particular numbers used for each day of the week. It would be far better if the user were able to type the actual day names in.

Consider the input of a DayOfWeekType. This will require a procedure which converts a string input to a matching enumerated value. In order to allow for the possibility that the value the user inputs does not match any of the allowed options, and to provide for the repeated asking of the user for a valid input, a new type needs to be introduced. This would have values equivalent to the seven valid days and an extra one, here called NullDay. This then means that the enumerated type variable can be set to NullDay each time the input is unsatisfactory. Requests for input can then be processed with a while loop controlled by this value.

In order to establish a new enumerated type allowing all the day names plus the extra one, a new type (called DayOfWeekExtendedType) is declared first, and then DayOfWeekType is declared as a subrange type of the enumerated type, as follows:

```
TYPE DayOfWeekExtendedType = (Sunday, Monday, Tuesday, Wednesday,
Thursday, Friday, Saturday, NullDay);

DayOfWeekType = Sunday .. Saturday;
```

The following code depends on the use of a further procedure, ConvertDay, which has two parameters. The first is a string type, the second is a DayOfWeekExtendedType. It simply converts a string to its equivalent in the enumerated type.

```
PROCEDURE ReadDayOfWeek(VAR RDOWday : DayOfWeekType);

VAR   lRDOWdayname : STRING;
      lRDOWday      : DayOfWeekExtendedType;

BEGIN
    WriteLn('Which day do you want?');
    ReadLn(lRDOWdayname);
    ConvertDay(lRDOWdayname, lRDOWday);
    WHILE lRDOWday = NullDay DO
    BEGIN
       WriteLn('Please try again');
       ReadLn(lRDOWdayname);
       ConvertDay(lRDOWdayname, lRDOWday)
    END;    {of WHILE}
    RDOWday := lRDOWday
END;    {ReadDayOfWeek}
```

This code uses ReadLn to read a string one or more times and converts it each time to its DayOfWeekExtendedType equivalent. Once a valid value has been returned, signifying that a valid input has been given, the DayOfWeekExtendedType value is converted to its DayOfWeekType equivalent.

The code for ConvertDay is:

```
PROCEDURE ConvertDay(CDdayname : STRING;
                     VAR CDday : DayOfWeekExtendedType);

BEGIN
    CDday := NullDay;
    IF CDdayname = 'Sunday' THEN BEGIN CDday := Sunday END;
    IF CDdayname = 'Monday' THEN BEGIN CDday := Monday END;
```

```
      IF CDdayname = 'Tuesday' THEN BEGIN CDday := Tuesday END;
      IF CDdayname = 'Wednesday' THEN BEGIN CDday := Wednesday END;
      IF CDdayname = 'Thursday' THEN BEGIN CDday := Thursday END;
      IF CDdayname = 'Friday' THEN BEGIN CDday := Friday END;
      IF CDdayname = 'Saturday' THEN BEGIN CDday := Saturday END
   END;    {ConvertDay}
```

This may appear to be a particularly cumbersome method of input, but it does enable some enhancements to the program to be made fairly easily, so that inputs of strings such as 'sun' or 'SUNDAY' can also be interpreted as correct.

The code which is required for the input of a month should be based on the same pattern. It is not given here, but is necessary for the exercise later. Note that the value NullMonth should be used as the extra value in MonthExtendedType.

EXERCISE 9.6

Convert the 'log' suite to work with the input of day and month names and their conversion to enumerated types as described.

The next step in adapting this program is to allow for the checking of possible input strings by declaring them in an array rather than having the literals in-built, as they were in ConvertDay and ConvertMonth.

The strategy is to declare a new array type which will hold an array of strings, indexed by the enumerated type (in the first example, DayOfWeekType), with the string containing the string equivalent of the enumerated type. In order to do this, the following type declaration is used:

```
TYPE DayStringArrayType = ARRAY[DayOfWeekType] OF STRING;
```

The code to generate the array is perhaps best used as a local procedure only, and reads as follows:

```
PROCEDURE SetDayString(VAR SDSdaystring : DayStringArrayType);

BEGIN
    SDSdaystring[Sunday] := 'Sunday';
    SDSdaystring[Monday] := 'Monday';
    SDSdaystring[Tuesday] := 'Tuesday';
    SDSdaystring[Wednesday] := 'Wednesday';
    SDSdaystring[Thursday] := 'Thursday';
    SDSdaystring[Friday] := 'Friday';
    SDSdaystring[Saturday] := 'Saturday';
    END;    {SetDayString}
```

This is then used in a definite loop with a control variable which steps through each possible value of the enumerated type. If the corresponding element of the string array matches the input string, then the parameter is set to the value of the control variable. If no match is found, then the value remains as NullDay, which is why the extended type is used.

```
PROCEDURE ConvertDay(CDdayname : STRING;
                     VAR CDday : DayOfWeekExtendedType);

VAR lCDdaystring : DayStringArrayType;
    lCDdaycount  : DayOfWeekType;

BEGIN
   SetDayString(lCDdaystring);
   CDday := NullDay;
   FOR lCDdaycount := Sunday TO Saturday DO
   BEGIN
      IF CDdayname = lCDdaystring[lCDdaycount] THEN
      BEGIN
         CDday := lCDdaycount
      END    {of IF}
   END;    {of FOR}
END;    {ConvertDay}
```

The equivalent code for the months is as follows:

```
TYPE MonthStringArrayType = ARRAY[MonthType] OF STRING;
```

```
PROCEDURE SetMonthString(VAR SMSmonthstring :
                         MonthStringArrayType);

BEGIN
   SMSmonthstring[January] := 'January';
   SMSmonthstring[February] := 'February';
   SMSmonthstring[March] := 'March';
   SMSmonthstring[April] := 'April';
   SMSmonthstring[May] := 'May';
   SMSmonthstring[June] := 'June';
   SMSmonthstring[July] := 'July';
   SMSmonthstring[August] := 'August';
   SMSmonthstring[September] := 'September';
   SMSmonthstring[October] := 'October';
   SMSmonthstring[November] := 'November';
   SMSmonthstring[December] := 'December';
END;    {SetMonthString}
```

```
PROCEDURE ConvertMonth(CMmonthname : STRING;
                       VAR CMmonth : MonthExtendedType);

VAR lCMmonthstring : MonthStringArrayType;
    lCMmonthcount  : MonthType;
```

```
BEGIN
   SetMonthString(lCMmonthstring);
   CMmonth := NullMonth;
   FOR lCMmonthcount := January TO December DO
   BEGIN
      IF CMmonthname = lCMmonthstring[lCMmonthcount] THEN
      BEGIN
         CMmonth := lCMmonthcount
      END    {of IF}
   END    {of FOR}
END;    {ConvertMonth}
```

EXERCISE 9.7

Step 1. Convert the 'log' suite to work with the input of day and month names and their conversion to enumerated types by matching values against a string array as described.

Step 2. The use of a definite (for) loop in ConvertDay could be considered inefficient, as searching continues even after the string which is being searched for is found. It would be more efficient to use an indefinite (while) loop. Convert ConvertDay to an indefinite loop.

Step 3. On the same basis, convert ConvertMonth to an indefinite loop.

This approach works quite adequately, but as it has been described so far, the benefits might only just be seen to balance the effort needed. The next step, however, involves a minor amendment to the program, but provides a great deal of further flexibility in its function. This is the extension of the checking so that several different forms of input can be recognised for the day name, or later on, the month name.

The algorithm used requires a two-dimensional array.

Two-dimensional arrays are declared in a similar way to the arrays used so far (which are technically called one-dimensional arrays). They differ from one-dimensional arrays in that they have two indexes.

A one-dimensional array can be envisaged as a single column of entries or a list, such as

January
February
March
April
May
June
July
August
September
October
November
December

These items are then accessed by an index, which indicates which entry you require. So, in the above example, month[5] is May.

The above representation might be better shown as below, bearing in mind that the first column, in bold, does not form part of the data, but is merely for reference:

1	January
2	February
3	March
4	April
5	May
6	June
7	July
8	August
9	September
10	October
11	November
12	December

The principle of a two-dimensional table is an extension of this idea, so that both rows and columns are indexed. In order to allow for data entry of the day name either in full or as an abbreviation, two possibilities could be allowed on each day. The data is stored as strings in capitals as the input string will be converted to capital letters before checking in the table to allow for a mixture of cases in the input.

Here, the first index is shown down the side, and the second index across the top:

	1	2
Sunday	'SUNDAY'	'SUN'
Monday	'MONDAY'	'MON'
Tuesday	'TUESDAY'	'TUE'
Wednesday	'WEDNESDAY'	'WED'
Thursday	'THURSDAY'	'THU'
Friday	'FRIDAY'	'FRI'
Saturday	'SATURDAY'	'SAT'

It is important to be clear in this table that the bold entries represent the values of the index, which in the first case is an enumerated type, and in the second case is the integer in the range 1 to 2. The entries in the table are strings. An individual entry can be referred to by both indexes, so that the entry with indexes [Tuesday, 2] gives the string 'TUE'.

The declaration of the two-dimensional array type is as follows:

```
DayString2DArrayType = ARRAY[DayOfWeekType, 1..2] OF STRING;
```

If an array is declared of a DayString2DArrayType, then its elements are accessed through the indexes, which are sometimes called subscripts. A local procedure SetDayString is declared with a single var parameter of type DayString2DArrayType.

Its declaration is as follows:

```
PROCEDURE SetDayString(VAR SDSdaystring : DayString2DArrayType);
```

The actual code of the procedure is as follows:

```
BEGIN
    SDSdaystring[Sunday, 1]    := 'SUNDAY';
    SDSdaystring[Sunday, 2]    := 'SUN';
    SDSdaystring[Monday, 1]    := 'MONDAY';
    SDSdaystring[Monday, 2]    := 'MON';
    SDSdaystring[Tuesday, 1]   := 'TUESDAY';
    SDSdaystring[Tuesday, 2]   := 'TUE';
    SDSdaystring[Wednesday, 1] := 'WEDNESDAY';
    SDSdaystring[Wednesday, 2] := 'WED';
    SDSdaystring[Thursday, 1]  := 'THURSDAY';
    SDSdaystring[Thursday, 2]  := 'THU';
    SDSdaystring[Friday, 1]    := 'FRIDAY';
    SDSdaystring[Friday, 2]    := 'FRI';
    SDSdaystring[Saturday, 1]  := 'SATURDAY';
    SDSdaystring[Saturday, 2]  := 'SAT';
END;    {SetDayString}
```

This array is then used by an adapted version of ConvertDay, which examines each element of the two-dimensional array to check whether it matches the upper case version of the input. This involves a nested pair of loops. The outer loop steps through the days. For each day, there is an inner loop, which steps through the possible spellings. If a match is found, then the value of CDday is set to the appropriate day (as an enumerated type). You will notice that definite loops are used, and therefore searching continues even after a match has been found, but the minor extra amount of time which is taken by continuing to search unnecessarily is probably outweighed by the simplicity of the coding used here.

The input is converted to upper case by use of the pervasive UpCase function which returns a char value which is the upper case version of the char it is given as a parameter. Characters which are not alphabetic are unaffected by UpCase. The pervasive function Length returns as an integer the length of the string sent as its parameter.

```
PROCEDURE ConvertDay(CDdayname : STRING;
                     VAR CDday : DayOfWeekExtendedType);

VAR   lCDdaystring  : DayString2DArrayType;
      lCDdaycount   : DayOfWeekType;
      lCDcharcount  : INTEGER;
      lCDcount : 1..2;
```

```
BEGIN
  SetDayString(lCDdaystring);
  FOR lCDcharcount := 1 TO Length(CDdayname) DO
  BEGIN
    CDdayname[lCDcharcount] := UpCase(CDdayname[lCDcharcount])
  END;    {FOR}
  CDday := NullDay;
  FOR lCDdaycount := Sunday TO Saturday DO
  BEGIN
    FOR lCDcount := 1 TO 2 DO
    BEGIN
      IF CDdayname = lCDdaystring[lCDdaycount, lCDcount] THEN
      BEGIN
        CDday := lCDdaycount
      END;    {IF}
    END;    {FOR}
  END;    {FOR}
END;    {ConvertDay}
```

The equivalent code to allow the checking of possible spellings of months has the following form:

```
TYPE MonthString2DArrayType = ARRAY[MonthType, 1..6] OF STRING;
```

The procedures SetMonthString and ConvertMonth will work in a similar way to their 'day' equivalents, and are left as an exercise for the reader.

> *EXERCISE 9.8*
>
> Implement the changes to the log suite described above.

9.5 A related problem – displaying a calendar

The next problem requires a program which uses the same 'base' library, but a different 'util' library. This is illustrative of the idea referred to at the start of this chapter that a 'base' library should contain routines of use in solving a range of problems in the application area, in this case dates, with the 'util' library containing code written for specific problems. Therefore the utilities library should be called calutil.

The new problem requires the program to accept a month and year from the user and then will display a calendar for the given month in the form of a typical wall calendar of the type many of us made at school.

Thus, a typical month might look as follows:

```
A calendar for December 2002
Sunday                 2    9   16   23   30
Monday                 3   10   17   24   31
Tuesday                4   11   18   25
Wednesday              5   12   19   26
Thursday               6   13   20   27
Friday                 7   14   21   28
Saturday          1    8   15   22   29
```

The main program will look like this:

```
PROGRAM calendar;
{
     Another program for Chapter 9 - More dates
     Displays a calendar for the nominated month of a year
     Written by AMC/MPW
     1:1:96
}
USES calutil, logbase, utils, crt;

VAR  adayno    : 1..7;
     aday      : DayOfWeekType;
     inmonth   : MonthType;
     inyear    : YearType;
     possdates : DateArrayType;

BEGIN
   ClrScr;
   Welcome;
   Explain;
   ReadMonth(inmonth);
   ReadYear(inyear);
   ClrScr;
   GenerateTable(inmonth, inyear, possdates);
   GenerateDays(possdates);
   DisplayMonthHeading(inmonth, inyear);
   DisplayMonth(possdates);
   Pause;
   Farewell;
   RestoreColour
 END.   {calendar}
```

The elements here which are not defined in logbase, and which therefore have to be defined in calutil, are:

```
TYPE DateArrayType = ARRAY[1..31] OF DateType;
```

This will allow the program to store an array of 31 dates, which represents every possible date in the month.

GenerateTable and GenerateDays will function exactly as they did in the diary program.

Explain, a procedure with no parameters, simply outputs an explanation of the function of the program.

```
PROCEDURE Explain;

BEGIN
   WriteLn('In this program, you are asked to input first a ');
   WriteLn('month, then a year. The program will then display a ');
   WriteLn('calendar for the month within the year chosen.')
 END;   {Explain}
```

DisplayMonthHeading will produce the heading for the calendar for the particular month.

DisplayMonth will display the days of the month, with each of the seven rows containing the day name and the numbers of each day of that name, spaced appropriately.

The interfaces for the two new procedures are as follows:

```
PROCEDURE DisplayMonthHeading(DMHmonth : MonthType;
                             DMHyear  : YearType);
{
     Pre-condition:       is sent data in a MonthType as the first
                          parameter, and data in a YearType as the
                          second parameter
     Action:              displays a message explaining that this is a
                          calendar for the nominated month;   for
                          example 'A calendar for September 2001'
     Post-condition:      none
}
PROCEDURE DisplayMonth(DMdates : DateArrayType);
{
     Pre-condition:       is sent data in a DateArrayType containing
                          each day of the month with days set
     Action:              displays the days of the month, with each of
                          the seven rows containing the day name and
                          the numbers of each day of that name, spaced
                          appropriately
     Post-condition:      none
}
```

Their implementations are left as exercises.

In order to write DisplayMonth, it is advisable to develop a procedure WriteTheDay, which has two parameters and will print on a single line all the day numbers for the given day of the week. It does this by using an array of all dates in the month (the first parameter), and a specified day of the week (the second parameter).

Written in formal terms:

```
PROCEDURE WriteTheDay(WTDdates : DateArrayType;
                      WTDdaychosen : DayOfWeekType);
{
     Pre-condition:       is sent data in a DateArrayType, representing
                          all the dates in a particular month, as the
                          first parameter, and a DayOfWeekType as the
                          second parameter
     Action:              displays the day of the month of every entry
                          in the DateArrayType where the day matches
                          the second parameter
     Post-condition:      none
}
```

This procedure works as follows:

```
PROCEDURE WriteTheDay(WTDdates : DateArrayType;
                        WTDdaychosen : DayOfWeekType);

VAR lWTDcount : INTEGER;

BEGIN
   FOR lWTDcount := 1 TO
       DaysInMonth(WTDdates[1].month, WTDdates[1].year) DO
   BEGIN
      IF WTDdates[lWTDcount].DayofWeek = WTDdaychosen THEN
      BEGIN
         IF (WTDdates[lWTDcount].Day <= 7) AND
            (WTDdates[lWTDcount].DayOfWeek < WTDdates[1].DayOfWeek)
         THEN
         BEGIN
            Write('     ')
         END;   {IF}
         Write(WTDdates[lWTDcount].Day : 5)
      END   {IF}
   END;   {FOR}
   WriteLn
END;   {WriteTheDay}
```

The outer loop steps through every date in the given month. If that date is on the day of the week specified as the parameter, then blanks are output as the first column on the calendar is to be blank. Then the day number is output in a field five characters wide. Therefore, for each pass round the loop, only days with the chosen name are selected and their numbers are successively displayed in numerical order. They appear on the same line of output because of the use of the Write procedure rather than a WriteLn.

DisplayMonth should ensure that all days of the week are displayed on different lines through the use of the GotoXY procedure with differing second parameters. For each successive day (that is each time round the loop), the second parameter of the GotoXY procedure should be increased by one.

EXERCISE 9.9

Step 1. Implement the program described above using calendar.pas on the disk, writing the various procedures such as DisplayMonth which have been specified. Test your program by displaying a variety of months. A sample solution is provided as calendar.exe on disk.

Step 2. Produce an alternative version of the calendar printing program, which generates a two-dimensional array with the first index being the day of the week, and the second index ranging from 1 to 6. Generate the contents of the array by putting, for example, the first Sunday of the month, either in the array element labelled [Sunday, 1] if the Sunday falls in the first week of the month, or in [Sunday, 2] if it falls in the second week. This is perhaps best done by working through the dates from the first of the month, putting them in the first week's elements, and then switching to the second week once a Sunday is reached.

(The reason that the second subscript goes up to 6 is that it is possible for a month to consist of parts of six different weeks. For example, if a 30-day month starts on a Saturday, then week 2 begins on Sunday 2nd, so weeks 3, 4 and 5 begin on 9th, 16th and 23rd respectively. Week 6 therefore includes Sunday 30th.)

EXERCISE 9.10

These exercises are designed to help you to test yourself on the knowledge which you should have acquired in reading this chapter and doing the previous exercises.

1. Describe how the elimination process could be used to determine all the prime numbers from 1 to 100. A prime number is one which can only be divided exactly by itself and 1. In other words, it has no other factors.
2. Explain the term 'subrange type'.
3. What is the minimum sensible number of values which can be used for a subrange type?
4. Explain why the order of the possible values given in the definition of DayOfWeekExtendedType important?
5. Why is a special procedure needed for the input of each enumerated type?
6. Why is a special procedure needed for the output of each enumerated type?
7. Explain the use of pred and succ.
8. What is a two-dimensional array?
9. Is there any limit on the number of dimensions of an array?
10. What rules govern the type of an array index?

10
The hotel revisited

Before tackling this chapter it is essential that you are able to do the following:

- use the Pascal environment to edit, compile and run
- design and use a test plan
- use a unit dependency diagram
- use selection statements
- write and use procedures and functions with parameters
- carry out arithmetic on real and integer quantities
- format output
- use definite and indefinite loops
- use subrange types
- declare and use records
- use arrays of one or more dimensions
- organise code sensibly into different units
- use enumerated types.

Before tackling this chapter you will have produced a utilities unit, completed in Chapter 7.

After tackling this chapter, you should understand:

- file handling with a file consisting of one component
- file handling for a text file.

No new items are added to the utilities unit during this chapter.

10.1   Understanding the previous hotel case study

In Chapter 4, you used ready-written code, in hotbase.pas, which you did not examine in detail, as the concepts behind it had not, at that stage, been introduced.

You will also recall that the case study itself was unrealistic in a number of ways:

- data was only held for one day
- data was lost when the program halts.

These two shortcomings will be put right later.

First, you need to understand how the data was held using the data structure defined in hotbase.pas.

```
UNIT hotbase;
{
     Hidden library for Chapter 4 - Hotel Booking
     Written by AMC/MPW
     1:1:96
     This is provided as a source file which should
     be compiled for use in the case study.
     At this stage, you need not be concerned to
     understand its contents
}
INTERFACE

USES utils;
{
     Number of rooms is declared as a constant
     so that it can be changed easily
}
CONST numberofrooms = 20;
{
     Type used to store room bookings
     Users need only be made aware of the data type to use -
     its exact nature is hidden
}
TYPE HotelData = ARRAY [1 .. numberofrooms] OF BOOLEAN;

PROCEDURE InitialiseHotel(VAR IHrooms : HotelData);
{
     Pre-condition:      current data is ignored
     Action:             sets all rooms to vacant
     Post-condition:     parameter is returned with all elements
                         (rooms) in the data structure set to FALSE
                         (for vacant)
}
PROCEDURE Process(Pchoice1, Pchoice2 : INTEGER;
                  VAR Proombooked: HotelData);
{
     Pre-condition:      first parameter must contain menu choice
                         second parameter must contain room number
                         selected
                         third parameter must contain current booking
                         data
     Action:             if the menu choice is 1 or 2, and the room
                         chosen is valid, this procedure carries out
                         the operation chosen (book or display) and
                         displays confirmation that this has been done
                         or that it cannot be done (1 of 3 messages).
                         If the room chosen is not valid, one of the
                         other two messages is displayed.
                         If the menu choice is 3 (for exit), no action
                         is taken.
                         If the menu choice is not 1, 2 or 3, a
                         message to this effect is displayed
```

```
        Post-condition:     on return, third parameter contains current
                            booking data updated by new booking if
                            necessary
}
IMPLEMENTATION

PROCEDURE InitialiseHotel(VAR IHrooms : HotelData);

VAR lIHcount : INTEGER;

BEGIN
   FOR lIHcount := 1 TO 20 DO
   BEGIN
      IHrooms[lIHcount] := FALSE
   END     {FOR}
END;   {InitialiseHotel}


PROCEDURE Process(Pchoice1, Pchoice2 : INTEGER;
                  VAR Proombooked: HotelData);
BEGIN
   IF IsInRange(Pchoice1, 1, 3) THEN     {start of IF 1}
   BEGIN
      IF Pchoice1 = 1 THEN     {start of IF 2}
      BEGIN
         IF IsInRange(Pchoice2, 1, numberofrooms) THEN
            {start of IF 3}
         BEGIN
            IF Proombooked[Pchoice2] THEN     {start of IF 4}
            BEGIN
               WriteLn('Sorry, Room ', Pchoice2,
                         ' is already booked')
            END   {of first part of IF 4}
            ELSE
            BEGIN
               Proombooked[Pchoice2] := TRUE;
               WriteLn('Room ', Pchoice2, ' is now booked')
            END   {of IF 4}
         END   {of first part of IF 3}
         ELSE
         BEGIN
            WriteLn('Sorry that is not a valid room number to book')
         END   {of IF 3}
      END   {of first part of IF 2}
      ELSE
      BEGIN
         IF Pchoice1 = 2 THEN   {start of IF 5}
         BEGIN
            IF IsInRange(Pchoice2, 1, numberofrooms) THEN
              {start of IF 6}
            BEGIN
               IF Proombooked[Pchoice2] THEN   {start of IF 7}
```

```
              BEGIN
                 WriteLn('Room ', Pchoice2, ' is currently booked')
              END   {of first part of IF 7}
              ELSE
              BEGIN
                 WriteLn('Room ', Pchoice2,
                            ' is currently available')
              END   {of IF 7}
           END   {of first part of IF 6}
           ELSE
           BEGIN
              WriteLn('Sorry that is not a valid room ',
                          'number to display')
           END   {of IF 6}
        END   {of IF 5}
     END   {of IF 2}
  END   {of first part of IF 1}
  ELSE
  BEGIN
     WriteLn('Sorry that is not a valid menu choice')
  END   {of IF 1}
END;   {Process}

END.   {hotbase}
```

The number of rooms is declared as a constant that is then used throughout the unit. Throughout the two case studies, this has been retained as 20, but it could be altered to suit the context. In a real situation, the room numbers may not run consecutively if, for example, the first digit of a room number indicated the floor on which it was situated. This variation on the problem will not be addressed at this stage, but is used in a later exercise at the end of the chapter.

The data is currently held as an array of twenty Booleans. InitialiseHotel therefore works by using a for loop setting each entry to false.

A function IsInRange is used, though in doing your work in Chapter 4, you were not aware of this. You have since incorporated this into utils yourself.

This is a useful shared piece of code because the room number must be in the range 1 to 20 (or whatever the value of numberofrooms is), and the menu choice must be in the range 1 to 3.

The procedure Process appears very complex, but is fairly straightforward in structure. It involves nested if statements within if statements to cover all the possibilities.

If the first choice 'Make a booking' is chosen from the menu, there are three options, which are controlled by the if statements. There are two possibilities if the room number is valid; either the room is already booked (signified by the array element being true) and so a message is displayed to this effect, or the room is not booked (signified by the array element being false) and so the array element is altered to true and a message is displayed to this effect. The third possibility is that the room number is not valid, and this should generate an appropriate message.

If the second choice 'Display a booking' is chosen from the menu, again there are three options. There are two possibilities if the room number is valid; either the room is already booked (signified by the array element being true) and so a message is displayed to this effect, or the room is not booked (signified by the array element being false) and so a message is displayed to this effect. The third possibility is that the room number is not valid, and this should generate an appropriate message.

10.2 Converting the previous hotel case study to a version which uses file handling

In order to overcome the problem that data is forgotten when the program halts, a file will be used to hold data. Later, the program will be adapted to hold more realistic data, but at this stage the program will simply be adapted so that it holds the array of 20 Booleans between runs of the program.

A number of new instructions are used when handling files:

A file in Turbo Pascal must have a type. This is declared in a type declaration such as:

```
TYPE HotFile = FILE OF HotelData;
```

This declares a new variable type HotFile that holds HotelData. The file declaration implies that the file will contain a linear sequence of components of the type specified. In this case study, only one piece of data, of type HotelData, is held in each file. The term 'linear sequence' implies that each time a Read takes place on the file, then the next component will be read. The current case study handles the whole array of twenty Booleans as a single user-defined type (HotelData), so this is read or written as a single component.

The type declaration allows variables to be declared as the given file type. Procedures that then handle the files should therefore have local variable declarations such as:

```
VAR lIHfile : HotFile;
```

The variable lIHfile is a file variable.

'Assign' is used to make the link between the file variable (present at compile time) with a real file name (of a file present at run time). The compiler can only verify that a file name that is used in a program is a valid one; it cannot know that a file will actually be present when the program is run. Because it is held outside the Pascal system, the file on disk is known as an external file. The Assign command requires two parameters. The first is an identifier for the file, which must be a variable of the appropriate file type. The second parameter gives, as a string, an external file name, that is the name of an actual file on disk. It can be preceded by a drive name and path name in standard Dos format.

A sample statement is:

```
Assign(Pfile, 'hotdata.dat');
```

This would be valid provided that Pfile is a valid variable of file type. If the file hotdata.dat already exists, then the variable Pfile is assigned to it, and the file can be read from or written to. If the file does not exist, then it can be written to only. If the file exists, but is not a file of the same type as Pfile, then problems are likely to occur at run time.

A file in Pascal can be open either as read-only or write-only. Consequently, a file cannot be altered without copying the whole file, altering those parts which you wish to change.

The command Rewrite creates and opens a new file using a valid variable of file type that has been assigned an external file name. Any file with the given name that already exists is deleted and a new empty file is created in its place.

A typical example is:

```
Rewrite(Pfile);
```

The command Write sends data to an open file. It requires two parameters. The first is a variable of type file, the second a variable of the type held in the file. For example:

```
Write(Pfile, Proombooked);
```

In this case, Pfile is a file of HotelData, and Proombooked is a variable of type HotelData.

The Write procedure is used rather than the WriteLn procedure. This is because WriteLn only has a meaning for text files (see later in the chapter). The Write command will output to file in a binary format. This means that if you try to examine its contents, through Dos for example, the resulting display will not normally be meaningful characters, as the contents are not stored in character form.

The Reset command opens an existing file using a valid variable of file type that has been assigned an external file name. For example,

```
Reset(lIHfile);
```

opens a file.

The Read command reads the next component of the contents of a file. The first parameter should be a file variable, the second should be a variable of the type of element of which the file is composed. For example,

```
Read(lIHfile, IHrooms);
```

In this case, because the file is a file of HotelData, the variable must be of type HotelData and one item of data of type HotelData will be read.

Note again that the procedure Read is used, as ReadLn is used only for text files.

In the previous version of this case study, it was assumed at the start of each run that a procedure InititialiseHotel was called, which would set all the rooms to 'vacant'. In the new arrangement, where data is held between runs of the program, InitialiseHotel will need to read the existing data from disk. This creates a problem the first time the program is run, because no such file will exist. It is therefore useful to create a program that will generate an initial data file in which all the rooms are marked as 'vacant'.

This device is a common one when writing and testing programs that handle files. Such programs can be particularly difficult to debug. Errors in the program cause the file of data to be corrupted. Changes are then made to the program to put right these errors, and these may well be successful. When the program is run again, however, it might go wrong again, this time not because of an error in the programming, but because the data it is attempting to read has been corrupted! Many such frustrations can be avoided if the data file is reconstructed before the newly corrected program is run again. It is therefore common, when developing file handling programs, to write a separate small program that generates initial files. This will then ensure (so long as this program is run) that each run of the program starts with the same data. Only when the program works consistently with this standard data is it tested with differing data.

It is also instructive, at this stage, to see a simple file handling program, albeit one that only outputs to a file.

In this case study, there is a program called hotsetup:

```
PROGRAM hotsetup;
{
      Utility program for Chapter 10 - Hotel Booking on file
      Generates an initial file with no rooms booked
      Written by AMC/MPW
      1:1:96
}
USES hotbase;

VAR  myfile  : HotFile;
     count   : INTEGER;
     entry   : HotelData;

BEGIN
   FOR count := 1 TO numberofrooms DO
   BEGIN
      entry[count] := FALSE;
   END;
   Assign(myfile, 'hotdata.dat');
   Rewrite(myfile);
   Write(myfile, entry)
END.
```

This program uses the definitions of HotFile and HotelData in hotbase, as well as numberofrooms.

```
CONST numberofrooms = 20;

TYPE HotelData = ARRAY [1 .. numberofrooms] OF BOOLEAN;

     HotFile = FILE OF HotelData;
```

The program hotsetup uses Assign to give an external name to the file to be referred to internally as myfile, declared to be of type HotFile. The Rewrite command opens the file. The Write sends the data held in entry, a variable of type HotelData, to the currently open file.

Before running the new version of hotel, therefore, it is vital to run hotsetup to generate the 'vacant' data.

In creating the new, file handling version of this case study, it is interesting to note that the main program, hotel, is not altered. The form in which data is held, and indeed whether it is held between runs at all, is hidden from hotel. The changes should be made to hotbase.

The new version of InititaliseHotel will appear as follows:

```
PROCEDURE InitialiseHotel(VAR IHrooms : HotelData);

VAR lIHfile : HotFile;

BEGIN
   Assign(lIHfile, 'hotdata.dat');
   Reset(lIHfile);
   Read(lIHfile,  IHrooms)
END;   {InitialiseHotel}
```

Rather than setting all elements of the array to false, this reads the array in from disk and sends it back as the parameter.

The procedure Process will also need to be changed so that when the menu choice is 3, and the user is hoping to quit, the values are first stored to disk, using the lines:

```
Assign(Pfile,  'hotdata.dat');
Rewrite(Pfile);
Write(Pfile, Proombooked)
```

These will output to disk the current data, passed as a parameter to Process.

10.3   Overcoming another problem of the previous hotel case study

In the previous hotel case study, there was an inelegant part of the program, namely that the room number had to be input even if the option chosen was '3' to exit.

This was designed in a particular way so that there was a consistent approach to calling Process with three parameters. At that stage of the book, the 'if' command had not been introduced, and so was not used in either the main program 'hotel' or 'hotutil' that was visible to the reader and included the procedure AskFor. Now that the if statement has been introduced and used many times, it is straightforward to ensure that when the choice '3' is made from the menu, the room number is not asked for, but is set to a dummy value, such as zero.

One principle of good program design that is often advocated is that each procedure should carry out a single task. It can be argued that the previous procedure AskFor, which accepts the inputs, actually carries out two tasks, so in preparation for further program developments, this will be split as part of the same exercise. Two new procedures, AskForOption and AskForRoom should be generated in place of AskFor. These will, of course, need to be defined in the interface and implementation of hotutil. The main program should then be altered, so that AskForOption is called, and then AskForRoom is only called if it needs to be. If it is not called, then you should ensure that the room number is given a dummy value.

> *EXERCISE 10.1*
>
> Alter the unit hotutil in the manner described and amend the main program accordingly.

10.4   Handling more realistic data

The case study can now be developed using many of the concepts that have now been introduced. In an improved version, this program will hold bookings for 20 rooms for the seven days of the week, and will record the name of the person booking the room.

In order to do this, the underlying data structure should be altered. In the top-down spirit of this book, consider first the main program under the new specification.

```
PROGRAM hota;
{
     Main program Chapter 10 - Hotel Booking
     Version which stores data between one use and the next
     Written by AMC/MPW
     1:1:96
}
```

```
USES hotautil, utils, hotabase, logbase;

VAR option, room: INTEGER;
{program variables to hold user's choices}

      day : DayOfWeekType;

      name : STRING;

      bookings: HotelData;   {this data structure type is defined in
                              'hotabase', with the same name as
                              before but a different data structure}
BEGIN
   Welcome;
   {
      initialise variable 'option' which is used to control loop
   }
   option := 0;
   InitialiseHotel(bookings); {now reads previous bookings from
   disk}
   WHILE option <> 3 DO
   BEGIN
      DisplayMenu;
      AskForOption(option);
      IF (option = 1) OR (option = 2) THEN
      BEGIN
         AskForRoom(room);
         ReadDayOfWeek(day)
      END;
      IF option = 1 THEN
      BEGIN
         AskForName(name)
      END;
      Process(option, room, day, name, bookings)
   END;   {WHILE}
   Pause;
   Farewell;
   RestoreColour
END.   {hota}
```

You will note that this main program is not very different from main programs that you have previously seen. The main differences are in the specifications of a few procedures.

Firstly, days of the week are handled properly by using the file logbase that defines the DayOfWeekType.

InitialiseHotel still uses the HotelData type, but this now has a new definition as a two-dimensional array of records. In order that an array of records can be declared, the record type is declared first in hotabase:

```
TYPE

Room = RECORD
```

```
        Booked : BOOLEAN;
        Name : STRING
        END;   {of RECORD}
  HotelData = ARRAY [1 .. numberofrooms, Sunday .. Saturday] OF Room;

  HotFile = FILE OF HotelData;
```

Because the second subscript of the HotelData type array is a subrange (Sunday to Saturday) of a type that is not pervasive, then hotabase must contain a uses clause for logbase, where DayOfWeekType is declared.

New or amended procedures are needed in hotabase, with the following definitions:

```
PROCEDURE InitialiseHotel(VAR IHrooms : HotelData);
{
        Pre-condition:      current data is ignored
        Action:             reads current room bookings from disk
        Post-condition:     parameter is returned with all elements
                            (rooms) in the data structure set to values
                            read in from disk

}
```

```
PROCEDURE Process(Pchoice1, Pchoice2 : INTEGER;
                  Pday : DayOfWeekType; Pname : STRING;
                  VAR Proombooked: HotelData);
{
        Pre-condition:      first parameter must contain menu choice
                            second parameter must contain room number
                            selected
                            third parameter must contain the day of week
                            selected
                            fourth parameter must contain the name in
                            which the booking is to be made
                            fifth parameter must contain current booking
                            data
        Action:             if the menu choice is 1 or 2, and the room
                            chosen is valid, this procedure carries out
                            the operation chosen (book or display), for
                            the chosen day and displays confirmation that
                            this has been done or that it cannot be done.
                            If the room chosen is not valid, one of the
                            other two messages is displayed.
                            If the menu choice is 3 (for exit), no
                            action is taken.
                            If the menu choice is not 1, 2 or 3, a
                            message to this effect is displayed
        Post-condition:     on return, fifth parameter contains current
                            booking data updated by new booking if
                            necessary
}
```

In the unit hotautil, there will be three procedures that ask for input data. Their formal interfaces will be:

```
PROCEDURE AskForOption(VAR AFOchoice : INTEGER);

PROCEDURE AskForRoom(VAR AFRchoice : INTEGER);

PROCEDURE AskForName(VAR AFNchoice : STRING);
```

The comments to explain their pre-conditions, actions and post-conditions are left as an exercise for the reader.

EXERCISE 10.2

Step 1. Use the main program, supplied as hota.pas.

Step 2. Write the unit hotabase, with the following definitions:

```
CONST   numberofrooms

TYPE    Room
        HotelData
        HotFile

PROCEDURE InitialiseHotel
PROCEDURE Process
```

Step 3. Write hotautil, largely based on hotutil, with procedures

```
DisplayMenu
AskForOption
AskForRoom
AskForName
```

Step 4. Write hotaset, an equivalent of hotsetup, which generates an initial file, with no bookings in the new file format.

Step 5. Compile and test the suite.

Step 6. Draw a unit dependency diagram of the suite.

With the main version now working, it is possible to develop the suite in a number of further directions, such as searching the data in an attempt to satisfy booking requests, booking for a number of days and recording deposits. The data display could also be enhanced to show various items in tabular form.

EXERCISE 10.3

Step 1. In order to fulfil a booking for a range of days, the program must accept an arrival day and a departure day. Note that the room is not needed for the night of the departure day. In this limited form of data representation, you are still only looking at dates in a particular week, and therefore the departure date must be strictly later than the arrival date.

To search for an available room, if any, you need to know the two dates, so these should be sent along with the booking data to the procedure that will search for an available room. This procedure will then return the room number which is available, or zero if no room is available for the specified dates. (An alternative would be to return two parameters, a Boolean to state whether a room had been found, and a number of a room to be used only if the Boolean is set to true.)

The search of the data may as well take place in room number order. Set a Boolean assuming the room is available, and step through each day specified, setting the Boolean to false if any of the days are booked for that room. If all requested days have been examined for a particular room and no existing booking has been found, then that room is available. There is then no need to search further.

The formulation of the algorithm suggests that the loop which steps through possible rooms should be an indefinite one (as we leave the loop if a suitable room is found), but that the inner loop is a definite loop as we look at every day that is requested.

Step 2. Alter the data structure to include an additional field for deposit paid (as an integer number of pounds). Note how little of the coding has to be altered to do this. Much of the code will pass around booking data irrespective of the actual data fields stored, and will not need altering even when the extra field is present.

Step 3. Develop a bookings display procedure that shows as much booking data as possible in table form. It should be possible, for example, to show room numbers down the left-hand side of the screen, day names across the top of the screen and grid entries that show the name of the person who has booked or a vacancy. Colour would be quite useful to distinguish headings, names and vacancies.

Step 4. Alter the program suite so that valid room numbers are declared as a subrange type. Ensure that all room number inputs are validated, and that the new type is accessed by all the other parts of the suite that need room numbers.

10.5 Text files

An alternative approach to storing the data in a file is to use a text file. Pascal provides the pervasive type 'text' which is an ASCII text file. Text can be output to a text file using the WriteLn procedure, and read back using the ReadLn procedure.

The fields of a text file will normally be written one at a time, the 'Ln' part of the WriteLn ensuring that the following output will be on the next 'line' of the file by sending an 'end of line' marker to the file. When a text file is then examined using software such as Dos, each separate output will be displayed on a separate line.

The use of a text file limits the types of output to those which can be sent to the screen, such as integer, char, string and real. A text file cannot, for example, hold the Booleans as described above.

The ReadLn procedure is used to read from a text file. The 'end of line' marker is used to recognise the separation between items in the file. For each successive ReadLn of a text file, the type of the data held in the file must match the expected type, otherwise an input error will occur.

In order to implement the hotel case study using a text file, the declarations in the new version of the 'base' file, which we shall call 'hotbbase', should be as follows:

```
TYPE

Room = RECORD
        Booked : INTEGER;
        Name : STRING
        END;  {of RECORD}

HotelData = ARRAY [1 .. numberofrooms, Sunday .. Saturday] OF Room;

HotTextFile = TEXT;
```

Notice that, in this situation, the 'Booked' field is an integer type, rather than the Boolean type which has been used so far. The value zero is to be used for 'available', and 1 for 'booked' in an equivalent way to the previous Boolean values. Boolean values are not used as they cannot be written to a text file. The pervasive Boolean type is, in fact, a special case of an enumerated type, and no enumerated types can be directly output as text.

The variable used in the programs to represent the file should have the type HotTextFile rather than HotFile.

When outputting a text file it is important to ensure that all the data is written to the file. Whilst calling the WriteLn procedure is enough to prepare text for storage on the file, Turbo Pascal, in common with many other programming languages, actually uses an output system called buffering. This involves storing items for output to disk in an internal memory so that data can be written more efficiently as blocks of data to disk. At the end of output, however, there may be part of a block which remains to be written. A close command will ensure that this block is written.

The program hotbset which generates the initial data file would therefore appear as follows:

```
PROGRAM hotbset;

{
     Program to generate data file for Hotel
     Text file version
     Written by AMC/MPW
     1:1:96
}

USES logbase, hotbbase;

VAR  myfile : HotTextFile;
     count : INTEGER;
     entry : HotelData;
     aday  : DayOfWeekType;

BEGIN
   Assign(myfile, 'hotdata.dat');
   Rewrite(myfile);
   FOR count := 1 TO numberofrooms DO
   BEGIN
      FOR aday := Sunday TO Saturday DO
      BEGIN
         WriteLn(myfile, 0);
```

```
            WriteLn(myfile, '')
       END
    END;
    Close(myfile)
 END.    {hotbset}
```

In the unit hotbbase, the procedure InitialiseHotel would need to read all the data in the file; it would therefore work as follows:

```
PROCEDURE InitialiseHotel(VAR IHrooms : HotelData);

VAR  lIHfile   : TEXT;
     lIHcount  : INTEGER;
     lIHday    : DayOfWeekType;

BEGIN
    Assign(lIHfile, 'hotdata.dat');
    Reset(lIHfile);
    FOR lIHcount := 1 TO numberofrooms DO
    BEGIN
        FOR lIHday := Sunday TO Saturday DO
        BEGIN
            ReadLn(lIHfile, IHrooms[lIHcount, lIHday].Booked);
            ReadLn(lIHfile, IHrooms[lIHcount, lIHday].Name)
        END
    END;
    Close(lIHfile)
END;   {InitialiseHotel}
```

The close procedure here ensures that the file is then available for another operation, which is likely to be the output to the file. Whilst this close might not be strictly necessary, once all the data has been read from the file, the file need not be kept unnecessarily open.

In the procedure Process, reference must now be made to HotTextFile rather than HotFile. Whenever a 'Booked' field is referred to, it should be accessed as a value of 0 or 1 rather than as a Boolean field.

The output to the file when the option to exit is chosen will read as follows:

```
Assign(Pfile, 'hotdata.dat');
Rewrite(Pfile);
FOR lProom := 1 TO numberofrooms DO
BEGIN
    FOR lPday := Sunday TO Saturday DO
    BEGIN
        WriteLn(Pfile, Proombooked[lProom, lPday].Booked);
        WriteLn(Pfile, Proombooked[lProom, lPday].Name)
    END
END;
Close(Pfile)
```

EXERCISE 10.4

Step 1. Implement the hotel bookings system as described using text files. The main program, which should be called 'hotb', will be identical to 'hota' except that references to files will be to 'hotbutil' (a copy of 'hotautil') and 'hotbbase'. Use Dos to check the contents of the file after running hotbset, and after running hotb and making a few bookings.

Step 2. Add an extra feature to the menu of the text file program so that a booking can be cancelled.

EXERCISE 10.5

These exercises are designed to help you to test yourself on the knowledge which you should have acquired in reading this chapter and doing the previous exercises.

1. Explain what is meant by a file variable.
2. Explain the parameters of an Assign instruction.
3. Explain which instructions must come before an Assign statement.
4. Explain the difference between Write and Rewrite.
5. How many parameters, of what type, are needed for a Reset command?
6. Explain the relationship of a field, a record and a file, giving the Pascal versions of these.
7. Explain why the program hotsetup is needed.
8. Which procedures were changed when the program was changed to handle a two-dimensional array, and why?
9. Explain the differences between the Pascal type text and a file of a user-defined type.
10. Explain in your own words the algorithm used to find a vacant room.

11

Solve your own problems

Before starting this chapter, you should be able to do the following:

- use the Pascal environment to edit, compile and run
- design and use a test plan
- use a unit dependency diagram
- use selection (if) statements with logical and relational operators
- distinguish between formal and actual parameters
- distinguish between value and var parameters
- perform arithmetic on real and integer quantities
- format output
- use functions and procedures
- use case statements
- use definite and indefinite loops
- declare and use records
- use enumerated and subrange types
- declare and use arrays of one or more dimensions
- declare and use files for permanent storage of data.

No new concepts are introduced in this chapter. A series of related case studies is offered as small projects, enabling you to show what you have learnt as you have worked through the previous eight case studies.

For each of these case studies you will

- be given a scenario, for which a Pascal program is required
- create suitable data structures for the problem
- design a menu and screens for the user
- create a Pascal unit containing the procedures and functions for performing the menu options
- create a Pascal unit containing utility procedures and functions
- write a Pascal program which meets the initial specification
- test the program and document the testing.

11.1   The overall scenario

This series of case studies relates to the once sleepy village of Summer Rising, where certain residents have suddenly decided that computers are needed to create a modern image in the village.

Thus, computers are being installed by every organisation from the Leisure Centre to the Women's Institute. Some have great visions of what can be accomplished by means of a small PC; others have more modest ambitions or are frankly sceptical of the benefits which can be achieved.

Five initial projects are being undertaken, and you are invited to choose one or more of them. On the surface, the projects appear to vary greatly, but when you examine them more closely you will notice a common theme. Data needs to be stored, in memory or on a disk file, as an array of records. The data will need certain manipulation, including adding new records, deleting and amending old records, and displaying various lists.

11.2 The case studies

11.2.1 THE LIBRARY

The Summer Rising Village Women's Club operates its own lending library. Members donate paperback books that they have read and no longer want, and other club members may borrow these books for 10p a week. Profits are donated to charity. The library operates as a very informal set-up, and relies on trust that books will eventually be returned.

The librarian would like a program to assist with record keeping for the library. At present she uses a record card for each book. When a book is donated, she records the title, author, type of book (e.g. crime, romance, adventure, humour, etc.) and the date of donation. When a book is borrowed, she writes on the card the date and the borrower's name. When a book is returned, the borrower pays the loan charge, and the card is marked to show the book has been returned. If a book wears out, it is thrown away and the card is removed.

The librarian says that she does not need to know who has borrowed a particular book in the past, but she would be interested in keeping a record of how many times a book has been borrowed. She does not want to computerise the financial side of the library yet, and is not even convinced that a computer will make record keeping any easier than her current card system. She would therefore like you to write a program to deal with a small sample of 10 books from the library. If it is successful, she will then ask you to extend the program to cover the entire stock of about 200 books.

11.2.2 THE LEISURE CLUB

The Summer Rising Holiday Complex also operates a Leisure Club, to enable members of the local community to use the sports facilities. There are various categories of membership:

Full – allowing full use of all the facilities at any time;
Off-Peak – allowing use of the facilities between 10.00 a.m. and 4.00 p.m. Monday to Friday;
Junior – for members aged under 18;
Swim – use of the swimming pool and sauna only.

At present, a card index is used to record members' details :

* name;
* address;
* telephone number;
* date of birth;
* membership number;
* type of membership;
* membership renewal date.

The manager of the Leisure Club would like to computerise the records. In particular, he would like to be able to produce lists of members in the various membership categories, as well as adding and deleting members and amending details such as addresses. He is keen to have a computerised system, and hopes that the second version of the program will also be able to produce lists of, for example, people whose membership will need renewing soon, or junior members who are nearly 18.

11.2.3   THE EVENING INSTITUTE

The Summer Rising Evening Institute offers classes in a variety of subjects during the winter months. It is intended to offer the following courses during the Autumn Term:

Tuesday

- Beginners Spanish
- Cake icing
- Basic car maintenance
- First aid
- Weight watchers.

Thursday

- Intermediate French
- Dressmaking
- Intermediate car maintenance
- Popmobility
- Classical guitar.

The Secretary of the Institute would like a computer program to assist with enrolment. She needs to record a student's name, address, telephone number and choice of course(s). A student may take a class on one or both evenings. She also needs to know a student's status, as the fee is reduced for Senior Citizens and under-18s. She would also like the program to display a list of the names of all students taking a particular course. It is anticipated that, in the future, more classes will be organised on the same or additional evenings.

11.2.4   THE CRAFT SHOP

The Summer Rising Knitters Co-operative produces hand-knitted garments from local wool, most of which are sold to holiday makers. At present, they knit cardigans in small, medium and large sizes for women, and age 4–6, 7–9 and 10–12 for girls. Unisex sweaters are available in the same sizes plus XL (extra large).

When a garment is completed, the co-operative manager tags it with a price and garment number. A record card is made out for each garment, recording details of the garment number, knitter's name, size, type (sweater or cardigan), price, and date. When the garment is sold, the date sold is also recorded on the card. At the end of every month, the cards of sold garments are removed and archived, and the knitters paid.

The co-operative manager would like you to write a program to deal with these records. The knitters continue all year, producing about 20 garments a month. 50–60 garments a month are sold during the summer months. The manager would like your initial program to deal with up to 10 garments, and simply to delete the records of sold garments at the end of the month. She would like to be able to display a list of details of stocks of a particular size and type of garment. Later, she would like you to extend the program to cover the entire stock, to display other information such as a list of garments still unsold after 6 months, and to store a list of sold garments.

11.2.5   THE HIRE CAR COMPANY

Mr. Watt A. Banga of the Summer Rising Motor Company hires cars to tourists visiting the area. He has a fleet of eight cars, but hopes to expand to 12 within the next year. During an eight-week period covering July and August, all bookings are for complete weeks.

At present, a record card is kept for each car. The information on the card includes the car's make and model, colour, registration number and year of registration. When a car is booked, the hirer's name and the booking number are recorded on the card. The hirer's full details are also recorded on a form which is stored elsewhere and filed in booking number order. When the car is taken out, the mileage is recorded on the card, together with details of any extras such as child seats or a roof rack. The mileage is again recorded when the car is returned.

Mr. Banga is keen to put this car database on a computer. Initially he would like the program to deal with bookings for just one week, but he hopes that you will later be able to extend the program to cover the whole eight-week summer season. He would like to produce lists of which cars are booked and which are available. He needs the facility to add further cars to the database, and remove one temporarily if it needs servicing or repairs.

The financial side of the business is dealt with by other systems, and need not be considered. He also has no wish at present to computerise the detailed forms which hirers need to complete.

11.3   The solution

Using the pattern of unit and program construction and the methods for solution developed in the earlier case studies, you should now be able to produce programs to meet the requirements outlined above. Guidelines for solution are offered below, or you may wish to develop your own strategy.

1. Decide what your program is going to do, and write an explanation in English of this, without using any Pascal terms. Prepare this specification as if you were giving a presentation to your customer, but at this stage you do not need to include any screen layouts. The sort of questions your customer might ask about the program are:
   - How will the initial data be generated?
   - What lists of information will you be able to display?
   - What will happen if you try to enter a duplicate record?
   - What will happen if you try to delete something which is not in the list?
   - How will your design allow for future enhancements or expansions?
   - Will there be any limits on the lengths of data fields?
   - Will the program always return to the main menu after performing an option?
   You may think of other questions, which will aid your thinking about the program design. The scenarios you have been given allow for a number of choices and variations, so you as a programmer will have to decide on the boundaries and limitations wherever the specification is not absolutely clear and unambiguous.
2. Devise suitable data structures (i.e. records and arrays) to contain the information relevant to your scenario.
3. Decide what will be offered in the program's main menu, and design a suitable screen for the user.

4. Design the further screens which will appear when any of the options in the main menu are selected.
5. Decide what functions and procedures you will need in the unit or units, and write a brief description of each, together with any pre- and post-conditions.
6. Draw a unit dependency diagram for the whole program.
7. Prepare initial sets of test data for the program. At least 20 will be required if you are to test thoroughly all the options. Don't forget to state the purpose of each set of test data.
8. Code the main program.
9. Write skeleton units, in which the interface sections are complete but the implementation sections contain mainly dummy procedures.
10. Ensure that the main program and the units will all compile, even if it may not yet be meaningful to run the program.
11. Complete the coding of dummy procedures.
12. Thoroughly test the finished program, retesting if and when any alterations to code have to be made.
13. Compare your finished program with the original specification, and make a list of any discrepancies. Make suggestions for future enhancements which would improve your program.

12

Further libraries – graphics and sound

Before tackling this chapter, you should have completed the case studies of the previous chapters, and be familiar with all the concepts introduced in them.

In this chapter, you are invited to explore some of the other features of Turbo Pascal. Turbo Pascal provides a number of standard units, which are contained in the file turbo.tpl and automatically loaded into memory when you load Pascal. These units provide a number of procedures and functions for manipulating the text screen, displaying graphics, and invoking Dos calls. A number of them will be described here, and it is hoped that you will continue your exploration of them by using the on-line help or consulting the Turbo Pascal manual.

12.1 Announcing your program

Procedures provided in crt were first introduced in Chapter 3. This unit includes a number of useful procedures for screen display. The procedures you have encountered already are:

- ClrScr
- TextColor
- TextBackground
- GotoXY

A series of constants is also defined in crt, linking colour names to the numbers 0 .. 15. The list of colours is given in Appendix 1.

In addition to manipulating the text screen, crt includes several procedures for creating sound. The sounds produced will not be up to the standard of modern computer games, of course, but you can create simple tunes quite easily. Procedures provided in crt are:

Procedure	Parameter	Description
Sound	Hz : WORD	Turns on speaker, at frequency Hz
NoSound		Turns off speaker
Delay	ms : WORD	Wait for ms milliseconds

Delay is not restricted to use with sound, and can be used to create a pause of a fixed time length, as opposed to the variable time length pause created when the program waits for the user to press the enter key. However, the 'millisecond' unit is very approximate, and may depend on the clock speed of your machine.

Different frequencies are used to produce sounds of various pitches: the bigger the frequency, the higher the pitch. The program below illustrates a simple alarm, with high and low pitched sounds alternating until a key is pressed.

```
PROGRAM alarm;
{
     Chapter 12 example
     Demonstration of the use of sound effects
     Written by AMC/MPW
     1:1:96
}
USES crt;

BEGIN
    WHILE NOT KeyPressed DO
    BEGIN
        Sound(400);
        Delay(500);
        Sound(200);
        Delay(500)
    END; {WHILE}
    NoSound
END. {alarm}
```

It is very important to include the procedure call NoSound at the end of the program, otherwise the program will terminate but the noise will continue! Note also the use of 'KeyPressed'. This is a Boolean function provided in crt, which returns 'true' when a character key is pressed on the keyboard. It does not detect keys such as Shift, Alt and NumLock. KeyPressed only detects that a key has been pressed, the character is not actually read but remains in the keyboard buffer for reading and further use if required.

The Sound procedure can be used with the frequencies of musical notes to play tunes. Repeated notes of the same pitch sound better if a brief break in sound is inserted. Middle C has a frequency of 512 Hz, and the octave starting at Middle C is:

Note	Frequency in Hz
C	512
D	575
E	645
F	683
G	767
A	861
B	967
C	1024

```
PROGRAM joyful;
{
     Chapter 12 example
     Demonstration of the use of sound effects to play a tune
     Written by AMC/MPW
     1:1:96
}
```

```
USES crt, ludwig;

BEGIN
    Bar1;
    Bar2;
    Bar3;
    Bar4;
    NoSound
END. {joyful}
```

The code which actually plays the tune is in the unit ludwig.pas.

```
UNIT ludwig;
{
    Utilities unit for Beethoven's 9th Symphony
    Written by AMC/MPW
    1:1:96
}

INTERFACE

USES crt;

PROCEDURE Bar1;
{
    pre-condition:      none
    action:             plays first bar of Beethoven's Ode to Joy
    post-condition:     none
}

PROCEDURE Bar2;
{
    pre-condition:      none
    action:             plays second bar of Beethoven's Ode to Joy
    post-condition:     none
}

PROCEDURE Bar3;
{
    pre-condition:      none
    action:             plays third bar of Beethoven's Ode to Joy
    post-condition:     none
}

PROCEDURE Bar4;
{
    pre-condition:      none
    action:             plays fourth bar of Beethoven's Ode to Joy
    post-condition:     none
}
```

```
IMPLEMENTATION

PROCEDURE Bar1;
BEGIN
    Sound(645);
    Delay(1000);
    NoSound;
    Delay(30);
    Sound(645);
    Delay(1000);
    Sound(683);
    Delay(1000);
    Sound(767);
    Delay(1000);
End; {Bar1}

PROCEDURE Bar2;

BEGIN
    NoSound;
    Delay(30);
    Sound(767);
    Delay(1000);
    Sound(683);
    Delay(1000);
    Sound(645);
    Delay(1000);
    Sound(575);
    Delay(1000)
END; {Bar2}

PROCEDURE Bar3;

BEGIN
    Sound(512);
    Delay(1000);
    NoSound;
    Delay(30);
    Sound(512);
    Delay(1000);
    Sound(575);
    Delay(1000);
    Sound(645);
    Delay(1000);
    NoSound;
    Delay(30)
END; {Bar3}

PROCEDURE Bar4;

BEGIN
    Sound(645);
    Delay(1000);
    Sound(575);
    Delay(1000);
```

```
      NoSound;
      Delay(30);
      Sound(575);
      Delay(2000);
   END; {Bar4}

   END. {ludwig}
```

It might not be quite what Beethoven intended, but it is just about recognisable.

EXERCISE 12.1

Enhance your Welcome procedure in utils.pas by adding your signature tune.

12.2 Text windows

The Window procedure in crt allows the user to define a window anywhere on the screen by specifying the coordinates of the top left (x1, y1) and bottom right (x2, y2) corners of the window. The default window is the entire screen:

Window(1,1,80,25)

Many crt procedures are relative to the current window, including ClrScr and GotoXY. The two functions WhereX and WhereY return the X (horizontal) and Y (vertical) coordinates of the current cursor position, relative to the current window.

12.3 Printer output

Turbo Pascal provides a unit called printer, which declares a text file called Lst and associates it with the LPT1 device. Using printer allows you to output from a program directly to the printer without any further declarations or coding, as the simple example below shows.

```
PROGRAM printit;
{
   Chapter 12 example
   Use of direct output to printer
   Written by AMC/MPW
   1:1:96
}
USES printer;

BEGIN
   WriteLn(Lst, 'This is how to output directly to the printer');
END. {printit}
```

EXERCISE 12.2

Write a program to output a printed list of Chapter 8's customers and their bank balances.

12.4 Dos utilities

Another unit provided with Turbo Pascal is the dos unit. This includes a number of useful procedures for setting and accessing the date and time and for file handling, as well as disk status functions and procedures for interrupt support and process handling. You have already seen how to access the system date, and the example below shows how the system time may be accessed. Many of the other functions and procedures would only be used in advanced programming, but are explained in the Turbo manual and in the on-line help.

```
PROGRAM timeis;
{
     Example for Chapter 12
     Demonstration of use of dos unit to access system time
     Written by AMC/MPW
     1:1:96
}

USES dos, utils;

VAR hour, minute, second, sec100 : WORD;

BEGIN
   GetTime(hour, minute, second, sec100);
   Write('The time is ');
   WriteLn(hour:1, ' : ', minute:1, ' : ', second:1, ' : ',
           sec100:1);
   Pause
END. {timeis}
```

EXERCISE 12.3

Reuse suitable procedures from the dates case studies to write a program which reads the system date and displays a message of the form:
    Today is Friday 2nd February 2001. It is the 33rd day of the year.

12.5 Graphics

Graphics programming can be great fun, and also very time consuming. The Turbo Pascal unit 'graph' contains a number of procedures for drawing lines and curves in various colours. It also includes several text fonts that can be magnified, justified, and oriented horizontally or vertically. In order to use graphics, the correct graphics drivers must first be loaded by calling the procedure InitGraph. The definition of it is

```
PROCEDURE InitGraph(VAR graphdriver, graphmode :   INTEGER;
                    driverpath : STRING);
```

A variety of graphics drivers is provided in the bgi directory supplied with Turbo Pascal; the third parameter must give the path to that directory as installed on your system. If the actual parameter for graphdriver is set equal to Detect, the appropriate graphics driver will be selected automatically. The program below draws some squares and circles on the screen and adds a caption.

```
PROGRAM graphit;
{
     Demonstration of use of graphics procedures for Chapter 12
     Written by AMC/MPW
     1:1:96
}
USES crt, graph, shapes, utils;

VAR  gdriver, gmode : INTEGER;
     midh, midv     : INTEGER;

BEGIN
   gdriver := Detect;
   InitGraph(gdriver, gmode, 'c:\pascal\tp6\bgi');
   SetBkColor(Black);
   midh := 300;
   midv := 200;
   DrawConcSquares(midh, midv);
   DrawConcCircles(midh, midv);
   SetColor(White);
   SetTextStyle(GothicFont, VertDir, 4);
   OutTextXY(500, 50, 'Sideways text too!');
   Delay(10000);
   CloseGraph;
   Pause
END. {graphit}
```

The unit shapes is given below:

```
UNIT shapes;
{
     Procedures for drawing shapes in graphics mode
     Written by AMC/MPW
     1:1:96
}
INTERFACE

USES crt, graph;

PROCEDURE DrawConcSquares(DCSmidh, DCSmidv : INTEGER);
{
     pre-condition:    DCSmidh and DCSmidv give coordinates of
                       centre of square
     action:           draws 15 squares in different colours,
                       midpoint (DCSmidh, DCSmidv)
     post-condition:   none
```

```
    }
    PROCEDURE DrawConcCircles(DCCmidh, DCCmidv : INTEGER);
    {
         pre-condition:      DCCmidh and DCCmidv give coordinates of
                             centre of circle
         action:             draws 15 circles in different colours,
                             midpoint (DCCmidh, DCCmidv)
         post-condition:     none
    }
    IMPLEMENTATION


    PROCEDURE DrawConcSquares(DCSmidh, DCSmidv : INTEGER);

    VAR lDCSlineColour, lDCSdist, lDCSdist10 : INTEGER;

    BEGIN
        SetBkColor(Black);
        lDCSlineColour := 1;
        SetColor(lDCSlineColour);
        FOR lDCSdist := 1 TO 15 DO
        BEGIN
            lDCSdist10 := lDCSdist * 10;
            Rectangle(DCSmidh − lDCSdist10, DCSmidv − lDCSdist10,
                      DCSmidh + lDCSdist10, DCSmidv + lDCSdist10);
            Delay(500);
            Inc(lDCSlineColour);
            SetColor(lDCSlineColour);
        END
    END; {DrawConcSquares}


    PROCEDURE DrawConcCircles(DCCmidh, DCCmidv : INTEGER);

    VAR lDCCcircleColour, lDCCradius : INTEGER;

    BEGIN
        lDCCcircleColour := 1;
        SetColor(lDCCcircleColour);
        FOR lDCCradius := 1 TO 15 DO
        BEGIN
            Circle(300, 200, lDCCradius * 10);
            Delay(1000);
            Inc(lDCCcircleColour);
            SetColor(lDCCcircleColour);
        END
    END; {DrawConcCircles}


    END. {shapes}
```

Most of the procedures used here are fairly self-explanatory.

SetBkColor sets the background colour, and SetColor sets the current drawing colour, using the same 16 colours you have already met in text mode. As with colours for text display, there is a choice of specifying the colour name or a numeric code. The colours are listed in Appendix 1.

Rectangle(x1, y1, x2, y2) draws a rectangle with its top left corner at (x1, y1) and its bottom right corner at (x2, y2). In the example program above, the coordinates have been chosen to make a square.

Circle(x, y, r) draws a circle of radius r, centred at (x, y).

The top left corner of the screen has coordinates (0, 0). The actual size of the screen depends on the graphics adapter being used.

The Write and WriteLn procedures are only available for text mode; the graphics alternatives are

OutText(textstring)

which outputs textstring at the current cursor position, or

OutTextXY(x, y, textstring)

which outputs textstring at (x, y).

SetTextStyle(font, direction, charsize) is used to set the font, direction (horizontal or vertical) and magnification of the text. In addition, text can be justified relative to the cursor position by a call to

SetTextJustify(horis, vert)

where horis can take the values: lefttext, centertext, or righttext; and vert can take the values bottomtext, centertext, or toptext.

Finally, a call to CloseGraph restores the screen mode to text and shuts down the graphics system.

During a program, you may wish to switch between text and graphics modes. This is easily accomplished by calls to

RestoreCrtMode – to switch from graphics to text mode, and
SetGraphMode – to return to graphics mode.

Note that SetGraphMode can only be used after a call to InitGraph.

EXERCISE 12.4

Use graphics to transform your Welcome screen into a work of art.

There are a number of other graphics procedures which have not been mentioned, and also several procedures for use in error detection and debugging. A detailed description of them is outside the scope of this book, but you are encouraged to explore the other contents of the Turbo Pascal units, using the on-line help descriptions as a starting point.

13
Further commands

This chapter describes a number of concepts in Turbo Pascal that were not introduced in previous chapters and are not essential in order to be able to complete the exercises in it.

These further ideas have been omitted earlier for one of two reasons.

Either:

They are instructions or constructs that allow you to do the same thing in a different way. The aim of this book so far has been to describe the minimum essential language for problem solving; these extra ideas are now introduced not primarily because they are better ways of doing things but because they are part of the language and you may see examples of their use which you would wish to understand.

Or:

They are instructions or constructs that are allowed by the language that we strongly suggest you do not use. Throughout this book, we have suggested many conventions of good practice. Many of these ideas are not essential parts of the language, such as the manner in which we have indented code or the way in which we have chosen identifiers, but they are ideas that we advise you to use. There are some concepts in Turbo Pascal, such as labels and local procedures, which have been included in many generations of programming languages. These are ideas that we advise you not to use, but when used appropriately they can be helpful. You will see such concepts used freely in some books and in some sample programs. It is therefore important that you understand the ideas whilst appreciating that good programming is better off without them.

13.1   REPEAT . . . UNTIL loops

Previously in this book, the only form of indefinite loop introduced has been the while loop, which has the following syntax:

```
WHILE <condition> DO
  <list of instructions>;
```

This program construct ensures that the list of instructions is executed while the condition, which must be a Boolean expression, is true. If, of course, the condition is false at the beginning, then the instructions are not executed at all. Because the number of times that the loop will be repeated is not determined before the looping commences, this construction is known as an indefinite loop, in contrast to the for loop, which is a definite loop. When while loops were introduced in Chapter 4, it was noted that if the condition is always true, then the loop will continue forever.

An alternative form of the indefinite loop is the repeat ... until loop. Its syntax is as follows:

```
REPEAT
    <list of instructions>
UNTIL <condition>
```

The condition must again be a Boolean expression. The list of instructions is executed in sequence until the condition is true.

The loop is again indefinite, as the number of times round the loop is not known in advance. The possibility again exists for the loop to continue forever. For this reason, you should again look out for confirmation that the condition is affected by the instructions within the loop.

Notice that the condition has the opposite effect to the condition in a while loop. A while loop is repeated while the condition is true. In a repeat loop, the condition being true is the signal for looping to cease.

One other very important difference between the two alternative forms of loop is that the repeat loop only tests the condition at the end of the loop. This is known as post-testing, as opposed to the pre-testing of the while loop. For this reason, the while is known as a pre-tested loop, and the repeat as a post-tested loop. Because the repeat loop is post-tested, the minimum number of executions of the instructions within the loop will be one, not zero as is the case with the while loop. It might be necessary, therefore, to test the condition before entering a repeat loop to ensure that the loop is not executed at all if the condition for termination is already true. This can lead to code which looks a little clumsy.

The main program in Chapter 4 could be adapted to use the repeat loop, as follows:

```
PROGRAM hotel13a;
{
     Main program for Hotel Booking
     Version using REPEAT loop
     Written by AMC/MPW
     1:1:96
}
USES hotutil, utils, hotbase, crt;

VAR option, room: INTEGER;  {program variables to hold user's
                                  choices}

    bookings: HotelData;    {this data structure type
                                  is defined in above}

BEGIN
   ClrScr;
   Welcome;
   InitialiseHotel(bookings);
   REPEAT
   BEGIN
      DisplayMenu;
      AskFor(option, room);
      Process(option, room, bookings)
   END
```

```
    UNTIL option = 3;
    Farewell;
END.   {of hotel13a}
```

This adaptation of the main program is included on the disk as hotel13a along with copies of the units as used before in Chapter 4.

Note that the variable option need not be initialised. It had to be initialised (to zero) in the form that used the while loop because its value was tested (by the while) before a value had been read in. In the new program, the value of option is set by AskFor before it is tested. This might be considered preferable, as the variable does not have to be set artificially.

Secondly, the begin and end within the repeat construction are unnecessary, as the repeat and until form an implicit blocking of the instructions between them. Note that for consistency the begin and end are included anyway. If they are omitted, the indentation is recommended for the sake of readability.

In the case of this program, the minimum number of times round the loop is one, which occurs when the user chooses 'exit' first time from the menu. There is therefore no problem in using the repeat loop. If the possibility occurred that the loop might need to be repeated zero times, then an if statement would need to be used:

```
IF NOT <end-condition> THEN
BEGIN
    REPEAT
    <list of instructions>
    UNTIL <end-condition>
END
```

This would ensure no execution if <end-condition> were true from the start. It would, of course, need to have a value in order that it could be tested.

EXERCISE 13.1

Re-write the function AreYouSure in utils using a repeat loop, and test that it works properly.

13.2   Local procedures and functions in programs

You have earlier been introduced to the idea of local procedures and functions in a library. Such procedures and functions, normally placed at the start of a library, can then be used by other procedures or functions within the library, but are not placed in the interface section and therefore cannot be accessed outside the 'sealed unit' of the library. The reason such procedures and functions are declared first is that when the unit is being compiled, their names can be placed in the dictionary of identifiers. When the compiler later reaches code that uses a procedure or function that has been declared locally, it will recognise the identifier. If an attempt were made to use the procedure or function before it was declared, then the compiler would produce an error message because it had discovered what is, at that point, an unknown identifier.

Local procedures and functions in libraries may be of some use. For example, if several different procedures in a library need to output a row of stars, or to ring the bell, then simple procedures could be written for this, placed at the start of the implementation, and accessed by several other parts of the library. This is what actually happens in Chapter 8. This idea can be explored by looking at the source code provided for Chapter 8. It could be argued, however, even in this case, that declaring such procedures in a separate library would be preferable, so that the code can be re-used by other programs.

The idea of local procedures in a program extends this idea. A program can be written with a series of procedures or functions in the main file. This would avoid the necessity of using libraries at all. In versions of Pascal which do not support units as Turbo Pascal does, such an approach is necessary. It does, however, undermine a lot of the principles of top-down programming, as useful procedures and functions then have to be copied to other programs rather than two programs sharing the same, carefully tested library.

The initial hotel booking program re-written using local procedures rather than libraries would look like this:

```
PROGRAM hotel13b;
{
    Main program for Hotel Booking
    Version using REPEAT loop and local procedures
    Written by AMC/MPW
    1:1:96
}
USES crt;
{
    Number of rooms is declared as a constant
    so that it can be changed easily
}
CONST numberofrooms = 20;
{
    Type used to store room bookings
}
TYPE HotelData = ARRAY [1 .. numberofrooms] OF BOOLEAN;

VAR option, room: INTEGER; {program variables to hold user's
                            choices}

    bookings: HotelData;

FUNCTION IsInRange(IIRvalue, IIRmin, IIRmax : INTEGER) : BOOLEAN;
{
    Pre-condition:      first parameter contains value to be checked
                        second parameter contains lowest value
                        allowed
                        third parameter contains highest value
                        allowed
    Action:             checks whether value given as first parameter
                        falls in the range declared by second and
                        third parameters
    Post-condition:     returns a Boolean function value of
                        TRUE if number falls in range
                        FALSE otherwise
}
BEGIN
    IF (IIRvalue >= IIRmin) AND (IIRvalue <= IIRmax) THEN
```

```
    BEGIN
        IsInRange := TRUE
    END    {first part of IF}
    ELSE
    BEGIN
        IsInRange := FALSE
    END    {IF}
END;    {of IsInRange}

PROCEDURE InitialiseHotel(VAR IHrooms : HotelData);
{
      Pre-condition:     current data is ignored
      Action:            sets all rooms to vacant
      Post-condition:    parameter is returned with all elements
                         (rooms) in the data structure set to FALSE
                         (for vacant)
}
VAR lIHcount : INTEGER;

BEGIN
    FOR lIHcount := 1 TO 20 DO
    BEGIN
        IHrooms[lIHcount] := FALSE
    END    {FOR}
END;   {InitialiseHotel}

PROCEDURE Choice1(C1choice : INTEGER;
                  VAR C1roombooked : HotelData);
{
      Pre-condition:     first parameter must contain room number
                         selected
                         second parameter must contain current booking
                         data
      Action:            carries out processing for choice 1 on the
                         menu. If the room chosen is valid, this
                         procedure carries out the booking operation
                         and displays confirmation that this has been
                         done or that it cannot be done (1 of 2
                         messages).
                         If the room chosen is not valid, a message to
                         this effect is displayed.
      Post-condition:    on return, second parameter contains current
                         booking data updated by new booking if
                         necessary
}
BEGIN
    IF IsInRange(C1choice, 1, numberofrooms) THEN
    BEGIN
        IF C1roombooked[C1choice] THEN
        BEGIN
            WriteLn('Sorry, Room ', C1choice, ' is already booked')
        END
```

```
         ELSE
         BEGIN
            C1roombooked[C1choice] := TRUE;
            WriteLn('Room ', C1choice, ' is now booked')
         END
      END
      ELSE
      BEGIN
         WriteLn('Sorry that is not a valid room number to book')
      END
END;   {of Choice1}

PROCEDURE Choice2(C2choice : INTEGER; C2roombooked : HotelData);
{
      Pre-condition:    first parameter must contain room number
                        selected
                        second parameter must contain current booking
                        data
      Action:           carries out processing for choice 2 on the
                        menu. If the room chosen is valid, this
                        procedure carries out the display operation
                        (1 of 2 messages).
                        If the room chosen is not valid, a message to
                        this effect is displayed.
      Post-condition:   none
}
BEGIN
   IF IsInRange(C2choice, 1, numberofrooms) THEN
   BEGIN
      IF C2roombooked[C2choice] THEN
      BEGIN
         WriteLn('Room ', C2choice, ' is currently booked')
      END
      ELSE
      BEGIN
         WriteLn('Room ', C2choice, ' is currently available')
      END
   END
   ELSE
   BEGIN
      WriteLn('Sorry that is not a valid room number to display')
   END
END;   {of Choice2}

PROCEDURE Process(Pchoice1, Pchoice2 : INTEGER;
                  VAR Proombooked: HotelData);
{
      Pre-condition:    first parameter must contain menu choice
                        second parameter must contain room number
                        selected
                        third parameter must contain current booking
                        data
      Action:           if the menu choice is 1 or 2, and the room
```

chosen is valid, this procedure carries out
the operation chosen (book or display) and
displays confirmation that this has been done
or that it cannot be done (1 of 3 messages).
If the room chosen is not valid, one of the
other two messages is displayed.
If the menu choice is 3 (for exit), no action
is taken.
If the menu choice is not 1, 2 or 3, a
message to this effect is displayed

Post-condition: on return, third parameter contains current
booking data updated by new booking if
necessary

```
}
BEGIN
   IF IsInRange(Pchoice1, 1, 3) THEN
   BEGIN
      IF Pchoice1 = 1 THEN
      BEGIN
         Choice1(Pchoice2, Proombooked);
      END
      ELSE
      BEGIN
         IF Pchoice1 = 2 THEN
         BEGIN
            Choice2(Pchoice2, Proombooked)
         END
      END
   END
   ELSE
   BEGIN
      WriteLn('Sorry that is not a valid menu choice')
   END
END;   {Process}


PROCEDURE Welcome;
{
```
Pre-condition: none
Action: displays a welcome message at the start of a
program
Post-condition: none
```
}
BEGIN
   WriteLn('Welcome')
END;   {Welcome}


PROCEDURE Farewell;
{
```
Pre-condition: none
Action: displays a farewell message at the end of a
program
Post-condition: none

```
}
BEGIN
   WriteLn('Farewell')
END;    {Farewell}

PROCEDURE DisplayMenu;
{comments left as an exercise}

BEGIN
   WriteLn('Do you want to:');
   WriteLn('1: Add a booking');
   WriteLn('2: Display bookings');
   WriteLn('3: Exit')
END;    {DisplayMenu}

PROCEDURE AskFor(VAR AFchoice1, AFchoice2 : INTEGER);
{comments left as an exercise}

BEGIN
   ReadLn(AFchoice1);
   WriteLn('Which room (1-20)');
   ReadLn(AFchoice2)
END;    {AskFor}

BEGIN
   ClrScr;
   Welcome;
   InitialiseHotel(bookings);
   REPEAT
   BEGIN
      DisplayMenu;
      AskFor(option, room);
      Process(option, room, bookings)
   END
   UNTIL option = 3;
   Farewell;
END.   {of hotel13b}
```

The code for this program is supplied on disk as hotel13b.

You will probably agree that this form of program is both more difficult to read and less flexible for the future. Any procedures or functions that you would then wish to use in another program would have to be copied and, perhaps more importantly, the dependencies of procedures or functions on other procedures or functions would have to be examined carefully. In the unit-based designs, we were always careful to compile the different units in the correct order because of such dependencies. In the 'single program' design, the relationship must be reflected in the order of the local procedures and functions so that those which depend on others come after them.

EXERCISE 13.2

Re-write the pins case study in Chapter 5 using local procedures and functions only.

13.3 Sets

Turbo Pascal allows the declaration of a set type. A set is a collection of values. The values in a set are called the elements. In normal set notation, curly brackets { } are used, but these have a different meaning in Pascal, so square brackets are used. A set is a combination of values chosen from a set called the universal set, which is the list of all possible values. A set can therefore contain some of the possible values, all the possible values, or none of the possible values, when it is called the empty set. The order of elements in a set is not significant, and two sets are equivalent if they contain exactly the same combination of elements. Elements in a set cannot be duplicated.

In Turbo Pascal, a set type is declared by listing all the possible values that could be held in the set. This list of values must contain no more than 256 possible values of an ordinal type, that is a type which is capable of holding only a countable number of values, such as integer, rather than types such as real. The type from which the list of possible values is selected is called the base type; because its number of possible values must be up to 256, it is usual to make the base type a subrange or a combination of subranges.

For example, the following are valid declarations of set types:

```
TYPE capitalletterset = SET OF 'A' .. 'Z';
TYPE letterset = SET OF 'A' .. 'Z', 'a' .. 'z';
TYPE season = (spring, summer, autumn, winter);
     seasonset = SET OF season;
```

A set is declared of a particular type as follows:

```
VAR choice : capitalletterset;
VAR choice1, choice2 : letterset;
VAR myseason : seasonset;
```

The variables can hold any combination of values from the base set, such as:

```
choice := ['B', 'F', 'G'];
choice1 := ['A', 'B'];
choice2 := ['B', 'A'];
myseason := [summer]
```

Relational operators can be applied to sets. Where set1 and set2 are sets of the same base type:

Operation	Explanation	Example
set1 = set2	is true if set1 equals set2; that is set1 and set2 have the same elements	set1 = set2 is true when set1 = ['A', 'B'] and set2 = ['B', 'A']
set1 <> set2	is true if set1 is not equal to set2; that is set1 and set2 do not have the same elements	set1 <> set2 is true when set1 = ['A', 'B'] and set2 = ['A', 'C']
set1 <= set2	is true if set1 is a subset of set2; that is every element of set1 is an element of set2	set1 <= set2 is true when set1 = ['A'] and set2 = ['A', 'B']
set1 >= set2	is true if set1 is a superset of set2; that is every element of set2 is an element of set1	set1 >= set2 is true when set1 = ['A', 'C'] and set2 = ['A']

Operation	Explanation	Example
element IN set1	is true if element is in set1	element in set1 is true when element = 'A' and set1 = ['A', 'B', 'C']

Operations on sets can be carried out on sets of the same type. There are three operations:

Operation	Explanation	Example
set1 + set2	generates a set which is the union of the two sets set1 and set2, yielding all the elements that are in set1, set2 or both sets	where set1 = [1, 3] and set2 = [2, 3], then set3 := set1 + set2 yields set3 as [1, 2, 3]
set1 * set2	generates a set which is the intersection of the two sets set1 and set2, yielding all the elements that are in both set1 and set2	where set1 = [1, 3] and set2 = [2, 3], then set3 := set1 * set2 yields set3 as [3]
set1 − set2	generates a set which is the difference of the two sets set1 and set2, yielding all the elements that are in set1 but are not in set2	where set1 = [1, 3] and set2 = [2, 3], then set3 := set1 − set2 yields set3 as [1]

One example, again from Chapter 4, where set notation could have been used is in the function IsInRange, which could be written as follows:

```
FUNCTION IsInRange(IIRvalue, IIRmin, IIRmax : INTEGER) : BOOLEAN;
{
      Pre-condition:      first parameter contains value to be checked
                          second parameter contains lowest value
                          allowed
                          third parameter contains highest value
                          allowed
      Action:             checks whether value given as first parameter
                          falls in the range declared by second and
                          third parameters
      Post-condition:     returns a Boolean function value of
                          TRUE if number falls in range
                          FALSE otherwise
}
BEGIN
   IF IIRvalue IN [IIRmin .. IIRmax] THEN
   BEGIN
      IsInRange := TRUE
   END    {first part of IF}
   ELSE
   BEGIN
      IsInRange := FALSE
   END    {IF}
END;    {of IsInRange}
```

The hotel case study could be implemented using sets rather than the array of Booleans described earlier. The full code of this, a further adaptation of hotel13b, is supplied on disk as hotel13c.

EXERCISE 13.3

Implement the function AreYouSure using set notation to determine whether an input is in the set

['y' , 'Y', 'n', 'N'].

Note that this will use a literal set rather than declaring a variable of type set. Test your new function.

```
PROGRAM hotel13c;
{
     Main program for Hotel Booking
     Version using REPEAT loop, local procedures and sets
     Written by AMC/MPW
     1:1:96
}

USES crt;
{
     Number of rooms is declared as a constant
     so that it can be changed easily
}
CONST numberofrooms = 20;
{
     Type used to store room bookings
}
TYPE HotelData = SET OF 1 .. numberofrooms ;

VAR option, room: INTEGER;     {program variables to hold user's
                                choices}
     bookings: HotelData;

FUNCTION IsInRange(IIRvalue, IIRmin, IIRmax : INTEGER):BOOLEAN;
{
     Pre-condition:      first parameter contains value to be checked
                         second parameter contains lowest value
                         allowed
                         third parameter contains highest value
                         allowed
     Action:             checks whether value given as first parameter
                         falls in the range declared by second and
                         third parameters
     Post-condition:     returns a Boolean function value of
                         TRUE if number falls in range
                         FALSE otherwise
}
```

```
BEGIN
   IF IIRvalue IN [IIRmin .. IIRmax] THEN
   BEGIN
      IsInRange := TRUE
   END    {first part of IF}
   ELSE
   BEGIN
      IsInRange := FALSE
   END    {IF}
END;   {of IsInRange}

PROCEDURE InitialiseHotel(VAR IHrooms : HotelData);
{
    Pre-condition:     current data is ignored
    Action:            sets all rooms to vacant
    Post-condition:    parameter is returned with all elements
                       (rooms) in the data structure set to FALSE
                       (for vacant)
}
VAR lIHcount : INTEGER;


BEGIN
   IHrooms := []
END;  {InitialiseHotel}

PROCEDURE Choice1(C1choice : INTEGER; VAR C1roombooked : HotelData);
{
    Pre-condition:     first parameter must contain room number
                       selected
                       second parameter must contain current booking
                       data
    Action:            carries out processing for choice 1 on the
                       menu. If the room chosen is valid, this
                       procedure carries out the booking operation
                       and displays confirmation that this has been
                       done or that it cannot be done (1 of 2
                       messages).
                       If the room chosen is not valid, a message to
                       this effect is displayed.
    Post-condition:    on return, second parameter contains current
                       booking data updated by new booking if
                       necessary
}
BEGIN
   IF IsInRange(C1choice, 1, numberofrooms) THEN
   BEGIN
      IF C1choice IN C1roombooked THEN
      BEGIN
         WriteLn('Sorry, Room ', C1choice, ' is already booked')
      END
      ELSE
      BEGIN
```

```
                C1roombooked := C1roombooked + [C1choice];
                WriteLn('Room ', C1choice, ' is now booked')
            END
        END
        ELSE
        BEGIN
            WriteLn('Sorry that is not a valid room number to book')
        END
    END;    {of Choice1}

    PROCEDURE Choice2(C2choice : INTEGER; C2roombooked : HotelData);
    {
        Pre-condition:      first parameter must contain room number
                            selected
                            second parameter must contain current booking
                            data
        Action:             carries out processing for choice 2 on the
                            menu. If the room chosen is valid, this
                            procedure carries out the display operation
                            (1 of 2 messages).
                            If the room chosen is not valid, a message to
                            this effect is displayed.
        Post-condition:     none
    }
    BEGIN
        IF IsInRange(C2choice, 1, numberofrooms) THEN
        BEGIN
            IF C2choice IN C2roombooked THEN
            BEGIN
                WriteLn('Room ', C2choice, ' is currently booked')
            END
            ELSE
            BEGIN
                WriteLn('Room ', C2choice, ' is currently available')
            END
        END
        ELSE
        BEGIN
            WriteLn('Sorry that is not a valid room number to display')
        END
    END;    {of Choice2}

    PROCEDURE Process(Pchoice1, Pchoice2 : INTEGER;
                      VAR Proombooked: HotelData);
    {
        Pre-condition:      first parameter must contain menu choice
                            second parameter must contain room number
                            selected
                            third parameter must contain current booking
                            data
        Action:             if the menu choice is 1 or 2, and the room
                            chosen is valid, this procedure carries out
```

                    the operation chosen (book or display) and
                    displays confirmation that this has been done
                    or that it cannot be done (1 of 3 messages).
                    If the room chosen is not valid, one of the
                    other two messages is displayed.
                    If the menu choice is 3 (for exit), no action
                    is taken.
                    If the menu choice is not 1, 2 or 3, a
                    message to this effect is displayed
      Post-condition: on return, third parameter contains current
                    booking data updated by new booking if
                    necessary

```
}
BEGIN
   IF IsInRange(Pchoice1, 1, 3) THEN
   BEGIN
      IF Pchoice1 = 1 THEN
      BEGIN
         Choice1(Pchoice2, Proombooked);
      END
      ELSE
      BEGIN
         IF Pchoice1 = 2 THEN
         BEGIN
            Choice2(Pchoice2, Proombooked)
         END
      END
   END
   ELSE
   BEGIN
      WriteLn('Sorry that is not a valid menu choice')
   END
END;   {Process}

PROCEDURE Welcome;
{
    Pre-condition:    none
    Action:           displays a welcome message at the start of a
                      program
    Post-condition:   none
}

BEGIN
   WriteLn('Welcome')
END;   {Welcome}

PROCEDURE Farewell;
{
    Pre-condition:    none
    Action:           displays a farewell message at the end of a
                      program
    Post-condition:   none
}
```

```
BEGIN
   WriteLn('Farewell')
END;   {Farewell}

PROCEDURE DisplayMenu;
{comments left as an exercise}

BEGIN
   WriteLn('Do you want to:');
   WriteLn('1: Add a booking');
   WriteLn('2: Display bookings');
   WriteLn('3: Exit')
END;   {DisplayMenu}

PROCEDURE AskFor(VAR AFchoice1, AFchoice2 : INTEGER);
{comments left as an exercise}

BEGIN
   ReadLn(AFchoice1);
   WriteLn('Which room (1 - 20)');
   ReadLn(AFchoice2)
END;   {AskFor}

BEGIN
   ClrScr;
   Welcome;
   InitialiseHotel(bookings);
   REPEAT
   BEGIN
      DisplayMenu;
      AskFor(option, room);
      Process(option, room, bookings)
   END
   UNTIL option = 3;
   Farewell;
END.   {of hotel13c}
```

EXERCISE 13.4

Step 1. Write a more general version of IsInRange which accepts two parameters, the first being the character input, converted to upper case if necessary, the second being a set of possible values which are accepted, irrespective of the case in which they are input.

Step 2. Write a new version of CheckPin which checks an input combination of char values against a set of possible values. (This is a more general version of the 'BOSS' version of CheckPin in Chapter 5.)

13.4 Other pervasive types

Turbo Pascal includes a number of extra types built in to the language over and above the types in standard Pascal. The standard type integer in Turbo Pascal allows numbers in the range -32768 to $+32767$.

The additional whole number types provided in Turbo Pascal are:

Type	Range of values
SHORTINT	−128 to +127
BYTE	0 to 255
WORD	0 to 65535
LONGINT	−2147483648 to +2147483647

13.5   Some other Pascal ideas which we do not recommend

Since Pascal was developed as a language for teaching programming over twenty years ago, much of the theory of programming has developed, encompassing top-down design, the use of units and object orientation. There are, however, a number of features in Turbo Pascal which, whilst they are available, are not recommended for use. More recent languages perhaps omit the parallel features. These ideas are included here partly as a warning against their use but perhaps also to enable you to understand other Pascal listings which you might come across which have not been written in the same carefully structured way as the code in this book.

13.5.1   LABELS AND GOTO

A line of code may begin with a label, followed by a colon. In standard Pascal, a label must be an unsigned integer of up to four digits. In Turbo Pascal, identifiers can also be used as labels.

A label can be used to start a line of code, and is then followed by a colon and the actual instruction. Labels were used in more primitive compiled and interpreted languages, and are still used in assembly languages to control looping, so that a conditional branch could be included, such as:

```
IF count < 10 THEN GOTO 55;
```

Modern high-level languages like Pascal render such coding obsolete because looping is allowed for by programming constructs such as while, repeat and case.

Where labels are used, they must be declared using the label declaration, which should precede the constant definitions. The declaration for the above use of 55 as a label would be:

```
LABEL 55;
```

Turbo Pascal gives a warning if a label is declared but is not used as a label to a statement. It is an error to attempt to use the same label to label more than one statement.

It is rank bad practice to use labels at all.

13.5.2   FORWARD REFERENCES

Previously reference has been made to the rule that a call cannot be made to a procedure or function before it has itself been declared.

There is one exception to this rule, which is when two procedures or functions are mutually recursive. The idea of recursive procedures and functions is beyond the scope of this book and involves the relationship, under controlled conditions, that each procedure or function can call the other. In this case, and this case only, the idea of a forward reference should be used. Unfortunately, the concept of a forward reference can be mis-used, and it is this mis-use only which we shall describe.

A procedure or function can be declared by giving the heading followed by the word forward. The full definition can then be given later. Some lazy programmers may not have a properly thought-out relationship between their procedures and functions. If a procedure or function early in the list of declarations makes use of a declaration later on, the code will not compile. The 'quick and dirty' solution to this problem is to declare that later procedure before the one which fails to compile, declaring it in a single line as a forward reference. The proper solution is to move the code to the correct place, which is perfectly easy to do.

The danger of using forward references to overcome this short-term problem is that you may end up with procedures or functions which both use each other when you did not mean this to happen. This implies therefore that very basic errors, of which you would wish to be informed, have been bypassed by your own laziness.

When writing recursive procedures and functions, however, forward references soon become important and unavoidable.

13.5.3   CONSTRAINTS ON FUNCTIONS

As defined in Turbo Pascal, functions cannot have a user-defined structured type. Functions must, of course, have some type, but the rules of Pascal limit this type to in-built or pervasive types or subranges of simple types. This can be a frustrating limitation, and is overcome in later languages like Modula-2, also designed by Nicklaus Wirth, who designed Pascal.

Functions can, however, be declared with var parameters. This would generally be viewed as a very bad practice. Functions are designed to be used in such a way that they return results and they are syntactically equivalent to an expression of their defined type. The use of var parameters within a function means that values of the variables passed as parameters to such functions may be altered by those functions. This could then have an impact on the rest of the program, or on the next call of that same function. The feature of using var parameters for functions has little practical use, particularly at this level of study, but has grave side-effects which work against the whole principle of top-down design which we have espoused in this book. The Turbo Pascal compiler will allow such use, which means that such a mistake could be made inadvertently.

13.5.4   ILLUSTRATING THESE INAPPROPRIATE FEATURES

The program hotel13d illustrates attempts to use each of the three features described in this section entirely inappropriately.

```
PROGRAM hotel13d;
{
      Main program for Hotel Booking
      Version using REPEAT loop, local procedures and sets
      It also uses gotos, forward references and functions with
      vars, all of which are not recommended
      Written by AMC/MPW
      1:1:96
}
USES crt;
{
      Number of rooms is declared as a constant
      so that it can be changed easily
}
```

```
CONST numberofrooms = 20;
{
     Type used to store room bookings
     Users need only be made aware of the data type to use -
     its exact nature is hidden
}


TYPE HotelData = SET OF 1 .. numberofrooms ;

VAR option, room: INTEGER;   {program variables to hold user's
                                choices}


     bookings: HotelData;    {this data structure type
                                is defined above}


PROCEDURE InitialiseHotel(VAR IHrooms : HotelData);
{
     Pre-condition:     current data is ignored
     Action:            sets all rooms to vacant
     Post-condition:    parameter is returned with all elements
                        (rooms) in the data structure set to FALSE
                        (for vacant)
}
VAR lIHcount : INTEGER;


BEGIN
   IHrooms := []
END;   {InitialiseHotel}


FUNCTION IsInRange(VAR IIRvalue : INTEGER;
                   IIRmin, IIRmax : INTEGER):BOOLEAN; FORWARD;

PROCEDURE Choice1(C1choice : INTEGER; VAR C1roombooked : HotelData);
{
     Pre-condition:     first parameter must contain room number
                        selected
                        second parameter must contain current booking
                        data
     Action:            carries out processing for choice 1 on the
                        menu. If the room chosen is valid, this
                        procedure carries out the booking operation
                        and displays confirmation that this has been
                        done or that it cannot be done (1 of 2
                        messages).
                        If the room chosen is not valid, a message to
                        this effect is displayed.
     Post-condition:    on return, second parameter contains current
                        booking data updated by new booking if
                        necessary
}
BEGIN
   IF IsInRange(C1choice, 1, numberofrooms) THEN
```

```
    BEGIN
      IF C1choice IN C1roombooked THEN
      BEGIN
        WriteLn('Sorry, Room ', C1choice, ' is already booked')
      END
      ELSE
      BEGIN
        C1roombooked := C1roombooked + [C1choice];
        WriteLn('Room ', C1choice, ' is now booked')
      END
    END
    ELSE
    BEGIN
      WriteLn('Sorry that is not a valid room number to book')
    END
END;   {of Choice1}


PROCEDURE Choice2(C2choice : INTEGER; C2roombooked : HotelData);
{
    Pre-condition:     first parameter must contain room number
                       selected
                       second parameter must contain current booking
                       data
    Action:            carries out processing for choice 2 on the
                       menu. If the room chosen is valid, this
                       procedure carries out the display operation
                       (1 of 2 messages).
                       If the room chosen is not valid, a message to
                       this effect is displayed.
    Post-condition:    none
}
BEGIN
  IF IsInRange(C2choice, 1, numberofrooms) THEN
  BEGIN
      IF C2choice IN C2roombooked THEN
      BEGIN
        WriteLn('Room ', C2choice, ' is currently booked')
      END
      ELSE
      BEGIN
        WriteLn('Room ', C2choice, ' is currently available')
      END
    END
    ELSE
    BEGIN
      WriteLn('Sorry that is not a valid room number to display')
    END
END;   {of Choice2}


PROCEDURE Process(Pchoice1, Pchoice2 : INTEGER;
                   VAR Proombooked: HotelData);
```

```
{
    Pre-condition:      first parameter must contain menu choice
                        second parameter must contain room number
                        selected
                        third parameter must contain current booking
                        data
    Action:             if the menu choice is 1 or 2, and the room
                        chosen is valid, this procedure carries out
                        the operation chosen (book or display) and
                        displays confirmation that this has been done
                        or that it cannot be done (1 of 3 messages).
                        If the room chosen is not valid, one of the
                        other two messages is displayed.
                        If the menu choice is 3 (for exit), no action
                        is taken.
                        If the menu choice is not 1, 2 or 3, a
                        message to this effect is displayed.
    Post-condition:     on return, third parameter contains current
                        booking data updated by new booking if
                        necessary
}
LABEL badinput;

BEGIN
    IF NOT IsInRange(Pchoice1, 1, 3) THEN GOTO badinput;
    IF Pchoice1 = 1 THEN
    BEGIN
        Choice1(Pchoice2, Proombooked);
    END
    ELSE
    BEGIN
        IF Pchoice1 = 2 THEN
        BEGIN
            Choice2(Pchoice2, Proombooked)
        END
    END;
    badinput : WriteLn('Sorry that is not a valid menu choice')
END;    {Process}

FUNCTION IsInRange(VAR IIRvalue : INTEGER;
                   IIRmin, IIRmax : INTEGER) : BOOLEAN;
{
    Pre-condition:      first parameter contains value to be checked
                        second parameter contains lowest value
                        allowed
                        third parameter contains highest value allowed
    Action:             checks whether value given as first parameter
                        falls in the range declared by second and
                        third parameters
    Post-condition:     returns a Boolean function value of
                        TRUE if number falls in range
                        FALSE otherwise
}
```

```
BEGIN
   IF IIRvalue IN [IIRmin .. IIRmax] THEN
   BEGIN
      IIRvalue := 0;
      IsInRange := TRUE
   END   {first part of IF}
   ELSE
   BEGIN
      IsInRange := FALSE
   END   {IF}
END;   {of IsInRange}


PROCEDURE Welcome;
{
    Pre-condition:    none
    Action:           displays a welcome message at the start of a
                      program
    Post-condition:   none
}


BEGIN
   WriteLn('Welcome')
END;   {Welcome}


PROCEDURE Farewell;
{
    Pre-condition:    none
    Action:           displays a farewell message at the end of a
                      program
    Post-condition:   none
}
BEGIN
   WriteLn('Farewell')
END;   {Farewell}


PROCEDURE DisplayMenu;
{comments left as an exercise}


BEGIN
   WriteLn('Do you want to:');
   WriteLn('1: Add a booking');
   WriteLn('2: Display bookings');
   WriteLn('3: Exit')
END;   {DisplayMenu}


PROCEDURE AskFor(VAR AFchoice1, AFchoice2 : INTEGER);
{comments left as an exercise}


BEGIN
   ReadLn(AFchoice1);
   WriteLn('Which room (1-20)');
```

```
      ReadLn(AFchoice2)
   END;    {AskFor}
BEGIN
   ClrScr;
   Welcome;
   {
      initialise all rooms to vacant
   }
   InitialiseHotel(bookings);
   REPEAT
   BEGIN
      DisplayMenu;
      AskFor(option, room);
      Process(option, room, bookings)
   END
   UNTIL option = 3;
   Farewell;
END.   {of hotel13d}
```

This program will compile successfully, but running the program shows up two of its errors.

Because IsInRange has been placed in the wrong place within the order (it comes after Process which uses it), the author has used the 'quick fix' of declaring it as a forward reference before Process, and then declaring it properly later. Unfortunately, this is allowed, and will not be shown as an error.

Because IsInRange has its first parameter as a var parameter, whilst the selection of the correct value true or false for the function is correct, the menu choice held by the main program is set to zero by the reference to the first formal parameter in the branch of the if statement in IsInRange. The correct actions are therefore not carried out.

Because a label is used within Process (and is therefore declared within it), the correct action does take place when an incorrect choice is made from the menu. Unfortunately, when the code input is valid, the error message is also output. The appropriate WriteLn statement used to be within the else branch of the if statement, but is now unconditionally executed.

These three specially generated errors are typical of the problems which programmers find when using forward references inappropriately, var parameters in functions inappropriately and gotos with labels, which are always inappropriate. It is probably apparent that these types of errors are very difficult to detect when you are attempting to debug a program.

EXERCISE 13.5

These exercises are designed to help you to test yourself on the knowledge which you should have acquired in reading this chapter and doing the previous exercises.

1. What is the minimum number of times a loop will be executed if it is:
   (a) a repeat loop
   (b) a while loop
   (c) a pre-tested loop
   (d) a post-tested loop?
2. What is the maximum number of times a loop will be executed if it is:
   (a) a repeat loop
   (b) a while loop

(c) a pre-tested loop
(d) a post-tested loop?
3. What are the maximum and minimum sizes of a set in Turbo Pascal?
4. Explain the terms 'intersection' and 'union' in set manipulation.
5. Why is a Boolean response the result of carrying out an 'in' operation?
6. Compare the relationship of integer to word with that of shortint to byte.
7. Why does the goto work against structured programming?
8. Why does the need for a forward reference often betray poor structured programming?
9. Why is it not advisable to use a variable parameter in a function?
10. What is structured programming?

14
Conclusion

You have now reached the end of the book and the course. If you have persevered and completed all the case studies, then you are well equipped to solve problems and write programs and also to continue to more advanced programming concepts. If you look back to the early case studies in this book, you will find that you have come a long way in programming since the start of the book. Programming is not an easy pursuit, but it can be intellectually challenging and enjoyable, and it is very satisfying to achieve the creation of a program which does exactly what it is supposed to.

There are several advanced programming concepts which this book has not covered. These include pointers and dynamic data storage, abstract data types, and the whole area of systems programming. The next step after an introductory programming course is often either an advanced Data Structures course, or another language. If you continue with an advanced course that uses Pascal, you will find that the next stages build on the firm foundation of the concepts and implementation of procedures and parameters, data structures and user-defined types that you have already established. On the other hand, if the next step is another procedural programming language, you should find that the concepts and structures you have assimilated will stand you in good stead. Try not to forget the good habits you have learned; short-term short cuts are often long-term long cuts.

The current enthusiasm in the programming world is for object oriented programming. This book has concentrated on ideas of structured and modular programming, concepts that have been established and developed over a number of years. Many of the ideas of object oriented programming are not new and revolutionary, but existing good practice dressed in a slightly different way. So if and when you do find yourself embarking on object oriented programming, do not be surprised to find that some of it has a familiar ring.

You are now equipped with a good basic toolkit which will enable you to write your own programs to solve your own problems. At the start of the book, you were invited to dive in. Now the time has come to strike out on your own!

Appendix 1   Pascal text mode colours

Colour code number	Colour	Colour code number	Colour
0	Black	8	DarkGray
1	Blue	9	LightBlue
2	Green	10	LightGreen
3	Cyan	11	LightCyan
4	Red	12	LightRed
5	Magenta	13	LightMagenta
6	Brown	14	Yellow
7	LightGray	15	White

TextColor may take values from 0 to 15, Black to White

TextBackground may take values from 0 to 7, Black to LightGray

Text can be made to flash by adding 128, or + Blink to the colour

e.g.   TextColor(14) or TextColor(Yellow) will give Yellow text
TextColor(142) or TextColor(Yellow + Blink) will give flashing Yellow text.

Appendix 2   Pascal conventions

Most large organisations insist on the use of coding conventions to avoid name clashes and to ease readability of code. In this book, we have used a series of conventions, but we have not 'taught' these as a concerted section of theory. It is our belief that readers will have acquired our conventions by reading code which we have supplied. Some readers may have discovered that various aspects work even when these conventions are ignored. We believe, however, that it is important for people learning programming to write readable, consistent code, and to acquire good habits from the start.

The conventions are described below.

Convention	Examples

Pascal keywords which are not procedure names should be shown in upper case	`BEGIN`
	`END`
	`PROCEDURE`
	`INTEGER`

A procedure identifier should begin with a verb (other than 'Is'), with the initial letter of each word in the identifier capitalised	`PROCEDURE InitialiseHotel` `PROCEDURE Process`
Pascal keywords which are identifiers of procedures or functions should be written with the initial letter of each word in the identifier capitalised	`WriteLn` `ReadLn`
A function identifier should have the initial letter of each word in the identifier capitalised	`FUNCTION MaxScore` `FUNCTION IsInRange`

Convention	Examples
A Boolean function identifier should begin with the verb 'Is' followed by an adjective or description of the condition	`FUNCTION IsValid` `FUNCTION IsInRange`

Formal parameters of a function or procedure should begin with the initial capitals of the procedure or function identifier, with the first letter of the remainder in lower case	`FUNCTION IsInRange (IIRvalue, IIRmin, IIRmax :`
	`INTEGER) : BOOLEAN;`
	`PROCEDURE InitialiseHotel (VAR IHrooms :`
	`HotelData);`

Local variables of a function or procedure should begin with a lower case 'l', followed by the initial capitals of the procedure or function identifier, with the first letter of the remainder in lower case	`PROCEDURE InitialiseHotel (VAR IHrooms : HotelData);` `VAR lIHcount : INTEGER;`
Program identifiers and unit identifiers should be no more than eight characters, entirely in lower case	`UNIT statbase;` `PROGRAM hotel;`
Constants should be written entirely in lower case	`CONST numberofrooms = 20;`
User-defined types should have the initial letter of each word in the identifier capitalised	`TYPE HotelData = ARRAY [1 .. numberofrooms] OF` `BOOLEAN;`

Comments of more than one line should have brackets on separate lines. Comments are indented by three spaces	`{`
	`   Number of rooms is declared as a constant`
	`   so that it can be changed easily`
	`}`

A program or unit should have an introductory comment giving a description, the author and date written	`{`
	`   Hotel Booking Program`
	`   Written by Alan Clark`
	`   9:7:95`
	`}`

A colon, equals or colon/equals should be	`VAR lIHcount : INTEGER;` `CONST numberofrooms = 20;`

Convention	Examples
surrounded by a space on either side	`IsInRange := TRUE;`
A relational operator should be surrounded by a space on either side	`IF Pchoice1 = 2 THEN` `. . . . .`
A declaration should be surrounded by a blank line before and after	`CONST numberofrooms = 20;`

All procedures and functions should show, in the INTERFACE, Pre-condition, Action and Post-condition as an initial comment	`{`
	`    Pre-condition:  current data is ignored`
	`    Action:         sets all rooms to vacant`
	`    Post-condition: parameter is returned with all`
	`                    the elements (rooms) in the data`
	`                    structure set to FALSE (for`
	`                    vacant)`
	`}`

Every 'END' should normally be followed by a comment explaining what it is the 'END' of	`END;    {of FOR}`
	`END;    {of IF}`
	`END;    {of InitialiseHotel}`
	`END.    {hotbase}`

An IF ... THEN or an IF ... THEN ... ELSE ... statement should include BEGIN and END around a set of statements even where there is only one command	`IF Mlist[lMcount] < lMresult THEN`
	`BEGIN`
	`    lMresult := Mlist[lMcount]`
	`END;    {of IF}`

A FOR or WHILE loop should include BEGIN and END around a set of statements even where there is only one statement	`FOR lCLcount := 1 TO listsize DO`
	`BEGIN`
	`    CList2[lCLcount] := CLlist1[lCLcount]`
	`END;    {of FOR}`

Indentation by three characters should follow a 'BEGIN' and cease with the corresponding 'END'	`BEGIN`
	`    FOR lHIcount := 1 TO 20 DO`
	`    BEGIN`
	`        HIrooms[lHIcount] := FALSE`
	`    END;    {FOR}`
	`END;`

Appendix 3   ASCII code table

Code	Character	Code	Character	Code	Character	Code	Character
0	NUL	32	space	64	@	96	'
1	SOH	33	!	65	A	97	a
2	STX	34	"	66	B	98	b
3	ETX	35	#	67	C	99	c
4	EOT	36	$	68	D	100	d
5	ENQ	37	%	69	E	101	e
6	ACK	38	&	70	F	102	f
7	BEL	39	'	71	G	103	g
8	BS	40	(	72	H	104	h
9	TAB	41	)	73	I	105	i
10	LF	42	*	74	J	106	j
11	VT	43	+	75	K	107	k
12	FF	44	,	76	L	108	l
13	CR	45	-	77	M	109	m
14	SO	46	.	78	N	110	n
15	SI	47	/	79	O	111	o
16	DLE	48	0	80	P	112	p
17	DC1	49	1	81	Q	113	q
18	DC2	50	2	82	R	114	r
19	DC3	51	3	83	S	115	s
20	DC4	52	4	84	T	116	t
21	NAK	53	5	85	U	117	u
22	SYN	54	6	86	V	118	v
23	ETB	55	7	87	W	119	w
24	CAN	56	8	88	X	120	x
25	EM	57	9	89	Y	121	y
26	SUB	58	:	90	Z	122	z
27	ESC	59	;	91	[	123	{
28	FS	60	<	92	\	124		
29	GS	61	=	93	]	125	}
30	RS	62	>	94	^	126	~
31	US	63	?	95	_	127	DEL

The printable characters have ASCII codes starting from 32.

Appendix 4   Pascal reserved words

The Turbo Pascal vocabulary includes a set of reserved words, in-built identifiers which have set meanings and may not be reused for other purposes. The reserved words are listed below:

ABSOLUTE	GOTO	RECORD
AND	IF	REPEAT
ARRAY	IMPLEMENTATION	SET
BEGIN	IN	SHL
CASE	INLINE	SHR
CONST	INTERFACE	STRING
DIV	INTERRUPT	THEN
DO	LABEL	TO
DOWNTO	MOD	TYPE
ELSE	NIL	UNIT
END	NOT	UNTIL
EXTERNAL	OF	USES
FILE	OR	VAR
FOR	PACKED	WHILE
FORWARD	PROCEDURE	WITH
FUNCTION	PROGRAM	XOR

In addition, Pascal has a set of standard identifiers. You can redefine these as your own identifiers, but you are advised not to redefine any that you might wish to use with their normal meaning, as confusion and errors are likely to ensue.

The standard identifiers include:

BOOLEAN	READ	WORD
BYTE	READLN	WRITE
CHAR	REAL	WRITELN
INTEGER	SHORTINT	

Index

Index to Pascal code in case studies

OWNERSHIP OF COPYRIGHT